OKLAHOMA!

The Applause Libretto Library Series

OKLAHOMA!

*The Complete Book and Lyrics
of the Broadway Musical*

Music by Richard Rodgers
Book and Lyrics by Oscar Hammerstein II

Based on the play *Green Grow the Lilacs* by Lynn Riggs

APPLAUSE
THEATRE & CINEMA BOOKS

AN IMPRINT OF HAL LEONARD CORPORATION

NEW YORK

Published in 2010 by Applause Theatre & Cinema Books
An Imprint of Hal Leonard Corporation
7777 West Bluemound Road
Milwaukee, WI 53213

Trade Book Division Editorial Offices
19 West 21st Street, New York, NY 10010

Photograph credits can be found on page 132, which constitutes an extension of this copyright page.

Printed in the United States of America

Book composition: Mark Lerner

Library of Congress Cataloging-in-Publication Data

Rodgers, Richard, 1902-1979.
    [Oklahoma! Libretto]
    Oklahoma! : the complete book and lyrics of the Broadway musical / music by
Richard Rodgers ; book and lyrics by Oscar Hammerstein II ; based on the play Green
grow the lilacs by Lynn Riggs.
        p. cm. — (The Applause libretto library series)
    ISBN 978-1-4234-9056-2
    I. Hammerstein, Oscar, 1895-1960. II. Riggs, Lynn, 1899-1954. Green grow the lilacs.
III. Title.
    ML50.R67O4 2010
    782.1′40268—dc22

                    2010008575

www.applausepub.com

For musical selections from *Oklahoma!*, visit www.halleonard.com.

A note on the dialect: Through his libretto and lyrics to Oklahoma!, Oscar Hammerstein II sought to capture the dialect of its specific time and place—Indian Territory, circa 1907. The language, therefore, was meticulously crafted and used as a guide for the original company of actors, who were well trained in elocution.

CONTENTS

FOREWORD

This series of librettos continues a fine tradition. Most of the plays and musicals that premiered on Broadway in the middle of the twentieth century were published in hardcover format. Random House led the way, but other publishers contributed, as well. With the Rodgers & Hammerstein musicals alone, for example, Knopf, Viking, and Farrar & Straus all participated.

These editions were always meant for reading. By design, they are not meant to be playing scripts. They lack vital information and guidelines needed to mount the shows, and they always carry with them a warning that the reader needs to go elsewhere to seek permission to stage the show or its elements. So if reading this libretto makes you want to sing a song or produce the show, please do note the process by which the official material can be found and the proper steps that should be taken—even in our Internet world—to do things correctly. The information can be found on page iv.

As one who, at a certain point in his life, collected the hardback editions of Broadway plays and musicals, I am thrilled that Applause has decided to take up the mantle of creating readable librettos of musicals. It is a tradition that needs to be encouraged! And all readers should know that this edition of *Oklahoma!* reflects, word for word, the edition that was first published by Random House in 1943.

Ted Chapin
The Rodgers & Hammerstein Organization
2010

INTRODUCTION

Oklahoma!—Where It Begins . . .

The words contained between these covers represent a revolution. Not a revolution in the historic, political, or military sense, but an artistic revolution of seismic proportions. And as is often the case, things were never the same once this revolution occurred.

Now, those may sound like lofty words, especially for what has often been taken as basically a musical comedy. To those who look at *Oklahoma!* and see a fairly simple story of farm girls, cowboys, and citizens of the "territory" wondering who will take whom to the box social, it is important to understand why this particular musical play has been heralded as the pivot point in the American musical. In a world of *Spring Awakening, Urinetown,* and *In the Heights,* the revolution of *Oklahoma!,* sixty-five years on, may seem a little quaint. But frankly, today we take for granted what this first Rodgers & Hammerstein collaboration gave us. Thanks to Applause Books, we now have an opportunity, for the first time in many years, to read *Oklahoma!* and begin to understand its revolutionary aspects.

Richard Rodgers and Oscar Hammerstein II came together to write *Oklahoma!* in a somewhat roundabout way. They met at Columbia University, where they were both students—but not at the same time. Hammerstein was seven years older than Rodgers. He lent an alumni hand to the annual Varsity Show when Rodgers was an undergraduate. Together they wrote three forgettable songs but at least had an opportunity to collaborate. Rodgers was already working with the person who was to become his exclusive partner for eighteen years: lyricist Lorenz Hart. Not too long after graduation, the team of Rodgers & Hart became a staple of Broadway, producing musical comedy after musical comedy. While these were always based on interesting ideas—from a musical of dealing with castration (*Chee-Chee*) to the story of a no-goodnik (*Pal Joey*)—the musicals of Rodgers & Hart are known ultimately more for their wonderful individual songs than for the shows themselves. Oscar Hammerstein II leaned in the direction of operetta, a popular form at the time, and started out working with a variety of partners. He and Jerome Kern created a masterwork in their 1927 epic *Show Boat*, but beyond that, the work that Hammerstein did in the 1920s and 1930s met with only middling success. While Rodgers & Hart were sailing along, Hammerstein was struggling.

In the early 1940s, the Theatre Guild, one of Broadway's premiere producing establishments, decided they wanted to create a musical from a play they had produced years before. That play was *Green Grow the Lilacs* by Oklahoman Lynn Riggs. They brought the idea to Rodgers & Hart. Hart, who was then finding the notion of doing any work increasingly difficult, expressed little interest in a musical of simple people set mostly outdoors. He had always been more comfortable in the sophisticated apartment-oriented world of "Bewitched, Bothered and Bewildered" and "The Lady Is a Tramp." Rodgers then spoke with Oscar Hammerstein, in whom he had confided his concerns about Hart. Hammerstein knew *Green Grow the Lilacs*, liked the idea of musicalizing it, and felt that his major collaborator Jerome Kern would be no more interested in the people of the "territory" than Hart was. So with the gracious assent of their partners, Oscar Hammerstein II and Richard Rodgers agreed to create the musical that the Theatre Guild asked for.

They set out to write the show they both felt was right. They spoke long and hard about what themes, people, and situations should be retained from the source material, and what should be added. They asked Agnes de Mille to choreograph, partly because they had been impressed with her Western-themed ballet *Rodeo*, and partly because she was interested in choreographing for the musical theater. Around them they assembled a group of collaborators with whom they had worked individually but who together formed almost a stable of creative partners for the future that ranged from director Rouben Mamoulian to orchestrator Robert Russell Bennett.

Although they may not have been completely aware of what they were achieving, they were taking all the innovations that they and others had been experimenting with through the prior decades and putting them all together in one show. As a result, they created a work that was both a popular success and one that the intelligentsia could recognize as being, for the first time, a unified work of American musical theater. As Rodgers explained it, "The costumes looked the way the orchestra sounded." Dance was an expression of character and situation. Song came out of spoken dialogue seamlessly. Story was told in words, action, music, and dance. The modern musical was born. And that was the revolution. Audiences filled 2,212 performances, making *Oklahoma!* the longest-running show in Broadway history for more than fifteen years.

If picking up this volume is your first experience with *Oklahoma!*, look at these words and imagine yourself versed not in today's sophisticated world, but in a more innocent world about to be changed forever by inevitable progress. Remember, *Oklahoma!* opened right in the middle of World War II. Agnes de Mille, the show's brilliant choreographer, explained that somehow within this show is the essence of America, of the country that we were fighting for then and must never take for granted now.

If you are well versed in the musical theater, then as you read this, think of the shows that came before. We can't ever feel the reaction today as viscerally as did those who experienced *Oklahoma!* in the 1940s. Henry Morgan, a radio and television personality whose zenith was around the time of this show, once explained to me how amazing it was that for the first time he could remember, "You didn't have someone march downstage to the footlights and belt out a tune and then step back into the stage setting to get back to the plot." I was in a meeting years ago when Jerome Robbins explain how fresh the whole show was, exemplified by the surprising "blue" note in the first song of the show. He said, "'Oh, what a beautiful *morn-'*—where did that surprising note come from? It really caught our attention and told us this was something very different."

Two great theater artists were at the core of the show: composer Richard Rodgers and librettist/lyricist Oscar Hammerstein II. Their collaboration proved to be fortuitous, as their combined voices created a new and unified kind of musical. Audiences responded positively. After *Oklahoma!*, they were here to stay. And stay they did: over the next sixteen years they created another eight musicals for Broadway, one television show, and one movie—and most of those remain popular today.

It is thrilling to see *Oklahoma!* back in print after many, many years. Musicals ultimately must be experienced in the theater to grasp fully what the creative artists intended. But as with any play, reading one gives us a good sense of what it can be. And in the case of *Oklahoma!*, it gives us an important look into the genius of these two men, Rodgers & Hammerstein. If they hadn't done their work as well as they did, you wouldn't be holding this volume in your hands today.

Ted Chapin

TIME LINE

January 26, 1931—The Theatre Guild presents Lynn Riggs' play
Green Grow the Lilacs on Broadway, where it runs for sixty-
four performances. A native of Oklahoma, Riggs drew from
his childhood memories of the Indian Territory's transfor-
mation into statehood for the historical context within his
play.

July 23, 1942—The *New York Times* reports: "The Theatre Guild
announced yesterday that Richard Rodgers, Lorenz Hart, and
Oscar Hammerstein II will soon begin work on a musical version of Lynn Riggs' folk-play *Green Grow the Lilacs*." Shortly
thereafter, lyricist Hart drops out of the project and Hammerstein takes over his duties. The resulting musical is the first in
the Rodgers & Hammerstein collaboration, which goes on to
yield such classics as *Carousel, South Pacific, The King and I,*
and *The Sound of Music.*

March 11–13, 1943—The new musical has its world premiere engagement at the Shubert Theatre, New Haven, Connecticut.
Titled *Away We Go!,* the work is termed "a musical play" with
book and lyrics by Oscar Hammerstein II, based on the play
Green Grow the Lilacs by Lynn Riggs, with music by Richard Rodgers. Presented by the Theatre Guild, it is directed by
Rouben Mamoulian and choreographed by Agnes de Mille,
with settings designed by Lemuel Ayers and costumes by Miles

White. The company includes Alfred Drake (Curly), Joan Roberts (Laurey), Betty Garde (Aunt Eller), Lee Dixon (Will Parker), and Celeste Holm (Ado Annie).

March 15–27, 1943—*Away We Go!* plays the Colonial Theatre, Boston, where changes are made prior to the show's Broadway premiere. One song is cut, "Boys and Girls Like You and Me." A second-act choral number, originally slated as a duet for Curly and Laurey, is introduced during the wedding scene late in act 2. Titled "Oklahoma," it stops the show.

March 31, 1943—With an exclamation point tacked on for extra flourish, the act 2 showstopper becomes the musical's title song when *Oklahoma!* opens at the St. James Theatre on Broadway to rave reviews.

- On December 2, 1943, Decca Records releases the original Broadway cast recording of *Oklahoma!,* marking the first time a musical is recorded complete with all members of the original cast, chorus, and orchestra; the album eventually earns a Gold Record and in 1976 is inducted into the NARAS (Grammy Award) Hall of Fame.

- On May 2, 1944, *Oklahoma!* receives a special Pulitzer Prize for Drama.

- On July 1, 1946, it surpasses *Hellzapoppin's* run of 1,404 performances to become the longest-running musical in Broadway history.

- On December 4, 1947, with Richard Rodgers conducting the second act, it gives its 2,000th performance on Broadway.

- On May 29, 1948, it closes on Broadway after a marathon 2,212 performances—a Broadway record unsurpassed until *My Fair Lady* in 1961—having been seen by more than 4.5 million people during the course of its five-year engagement.

- On May 31, 1948, the Broadway company of *Oklahoma!* embarks upon a yearlong tour throughout the United States, visiting sixty-seven cities.

October 15, 1943—The national tour of *Oklahoma!* opens at the Shubert Theatre, New Haven, Connecticut. It closes ten and a half years later at the Shubert Theatre, Philadelphia.

- During its decade-plus run, the touring company visits more than 250 cities encompassing every state in the Union before a total audience of 10 million.

- On November 26, 1946, the tour plays Oklahoma for the first time, and Governor Robert S. Kerr turns the event into a statewide celebration. Rodgers, Hammerstein, their wives, and members of the musical's creative and production team attend the festivities, which include balls and parades and culminate in eight sold-out performances of *Oklahoma!* in the Oklahoma City Municipal Auditorium.

- On August 31, 1953, less than five years after the musical has closed on Broadway, *Oklahoma!* returns to New York for a one-week run at the New York City Center. With its arrival, *Oklahoma!* joins three other Rodgers & Hammerstein musicals already running on Broadway—*South Pacific*, *The King and I*, and *Me and Juliet*—prompting Mayor Vincent R. Impellitteri to declare "Rodgers & Hammerstein Week."

February 26, 1945—USO Camp Shows, Inc., under the supervision of Reginald and Ted Hammerstein (brother and cousin respectively to the librettist), launches a nine-month tour of *Oklahoma!*, playing to the U.S. armed forces stationed in the Pacific.

April 29, 1947—*Oklahoma!* opens at the Theatre Royal, Drury Lane, London, with Harold (later Howard) Keel and Betty Jane Watson in the leading roles. Before it closes on October 21, 1950, *Oklahoma!* gives 1,548 performances in London, the longest run of any show in the 267-year history of the Drury Lane.

April 28, 1953—The Oklahoma State House of Representatives passes House Bill No. 1094, declaring the song "Oklahoma" by Richard Rodgers and Oscar Hammerstein II to be "the official song and anthem of the State of Oklahoma." The Senate ratifies the bill on May 6, 1953.

June 20, 1955—The American National Theatre and Academy (ANTA) "Salute to France" presents *Oklahoma!* at the Théatre des Champs-Elysées, Paris. Jack Cassidy (Curly), Shirley Jones (Laurey), and Pamela Britton (Ado Annie) star in the production, which follows its Paris engagement with performances in Rome, Naples, Milan, and Venice.

August 21, 1955—Shirley Jones, Ed Sullivan, Eddie Fisher, Richard Rodgers, Oscar Hammerstein II, and the governors of New York and Oklahoma lead an "*Oklahoma!* Song-Fest" at the Central Park Mall in New York before a crowd of fifteen thousand.

October 11, 1955—The motion picture version of *Oklahoma!* is released. Presented by Rodgers & Hammerstein and directed by Fred Zinnemann, it stars Gordon MacRae and Shirley Jones.

- The film receives two Academy Awards, for Best Scoring of a Musical Film and Best Sound Recording.

- It lives on in numerous theatrical re-releases, as well as repeated television broadcasts.

- A huge success on both home video and DVD, the film is given a special fiftieth-anniversary DVD release in 2005 when Twentieth Century Fox Home Entertainment releases a two-disc edition featuring *Oklahoma!* in both its Todd-AO and CinemaScope formats.

January 10, 1968—To celebrate the twenty-fifth anniversary of the musical play *Oklahoma!*, as well as the sixtieth anniversary of the state of Oklahoma, Governor Dewey F. Bartlett announces the formation of an honorary commission of nationally recognized leaders in the public arts, the academic world, and the business community to oversee events and commemorations pertaining to both anniversaries. Among those serving on the commission are Ed Sullivan, Leonard Bernstein, Darryl Zanuck, Walter Cronkite, Johnny Carson, Fred Astaire, Mary Martin, Jack Benny, William Paley, Jackie Robinson, Perle Mesta, Chet Huntley, David Brinkley, Harry Belafonte, Art Buchwald, Maria Tallchief, Will Rogers Jr., and Celeste Holm.

March 26, 1968—At Philharmonic (now Avery Fisher) Hall, Lincoln Center, in New York City, Skitch Henderson and Richard Rodgers conduct the New York Philharmonic Symphony Orchestra and an all-star cast in a silver anniversary concert version of *Oklahoma!* Staged by William Hammerstein, the evening features John Davidson (Curly), Constance Towers (Laurey), Anita Gillette (Ado Annie), Joseph Bova (Will Parker), and Margaret Hamilton (Aunt Eller).

May 1, 1979—A full-scale revival of *Oklahoma!*, under the direction of William Hammerstein, begins a cross-country national tour at the Pantages Theatre in Los Angeles. Tour sites include Washington, D.C.'s Kennedy Center and Oklahoma City, where, at the invitation of Governor George Nigh, *Oklahoma!* is presented in honor of the state's seventy-second anniversary of statehood.

- On December 13, 1979, with Governor Nigh in attendance, this production opens at the Palace Theatre on Broadway, where it plays until August 24, 1980, for a total of 293 performances, before going out on a post-Broadway national tour.

- The Broadway cast includes Laurence Guittard (Curly), Christine Andreas (Laurey), Mary Wickes (Aunt Eller), Harry Groener (Will Parker), and Christine Ebersole (Ado Annie).

- When Richard Rodgers dies on December 30, 1979, special tributes are centered around *Oklahoma!* (and the marquee is darkened in tribute), commemorating the last Rodgers musical to be playing on Broadway in his lifetime.

September 17, 1980—While the William Hammerstein production of *Oklahoma!* continues at the Palace Theatre on Broadway, a production directed by his brother James Hammerstein opens at the Palace Theatre, London, coproduced by Emile Littler and Cameron Mackintosh, starring John Diedrich as Curly, with Alfred Molina as Jud Fry. Following its London season, this *Oklahoma!* tours Australia in 1982.

October 3, 1990—Williamson Music, the music publishing subsidiary of Rodgers & Hammerstein, enters into an agreement with the state of Oklahoma, granting the state the right to use the song "Oklahoma" in the promotion of tourism. Waiving standard fees, Williamson Music charges the state of Oklahoma one dollar. The agreement is announced in Washington, D.C., by U.S. Senator David L. Boren of Oklahoma. Joining him for the announcement are Mary Rodgers, daughter of the composer, and William Hammerstein, son of the lyricist.

March 30, 1993—The U.S. Postal Service issues a stamp commemorating *Oklahoma!*—the first Broadway musical to be so honored. The first-day issue ceremony is held in Oklahoma City, and the stamp goes on sale that day statewide.

March 31, 1993—Fifty years to the day of its Broadway premiere, *Oklahoma!* and its cast alumni are saluted at a luncheon in New York City's Rainbow Room attended by more than three hundred guests. Eighteen members of the original company, including choreographer Agnes de Mille, conductor Jay Blackton, and leads Celeste Holm and Joan Roberts, are honored, along with representatives of the Broadway company (1943–48), the national tour (1943–54), the original London cast (1947–50), the movie (1955), the Lincoln Center revival (1967), and the Broadway revival (1979). At the luncheon, U.S. Postmaster General Marvin T. Runyon issues the *Oklahoma!* stamp for national release. New York City Mayor David Dinkins declares the day "Rodgers & Hammerstein Day" and renames the theater district block of Forty-forth Street between Broadway and Eighth Avenue "Rodgers & Hammerstein Row."

June 6, 1993—In recognition of its fiftieth anniversary, *Oklahoma!* is presented with a special Tony Award at the annual Broadway awards ceremony.

August 15–17, 1993: During the National Governors Association's annual meeting, held in Tulsa, Oklahoma, and featuring special guests President Bill Clinton and Vice President Al Gore, conference events honor *Oklahoma!* as the great American musical in its fiftieth-anniversary year. A delegation of U.S. governors attends a special performance of *Oklahoma!* at Discoveryland!, an outdoor theater that presents the musical every summer, joined by Mary Rodgers and William Hammerstein. Even the local Coca-cola bottling plant gets into the act, creating special *Oklahoma!/*Coca-Cola commemorative bottles.

July 15, 1998—A new production of *Oklahoma!* is premiered at the Royal National Theatre (RNT), London. Directed by Trevor Nunn and choreographed by Susan Stroman, it features Hugh Jackman as Curly, Josefina Gabrielle as Laurey, Maureen Lipman as Aunt Eller, and Shuler Hensley as Jud Fry. The production is an instant success with critics and the public alike; box-office records are broken for four consecutive days following the opening, and less than a month into the three-month limited run, the entire engagement is sold out.

- During the RNT engagement, the Queen Mother Elizabeth attends *Oklahoma!* on her ninety-eighth birthday, joined by Princess Margaret and members of the court, and is serenaded by the cast at the finale.

- In January 1999, Sir Cameron Mackintosh transfers *Oklahoma!* to the Lyceum Theatre in London's West End for a twenty-three-week limited season.

- *Oklahoma!* goes on to win a host of London theater awards, including the Evening Standard and Critics Circle awards for Best Musical and four Olivier Awards including Best Musical Production.

- In April, Queen Elizabeth II and Prince Philip attend a performance, joined by Mary Rodgers and Henry Guettel.

- In September, a film version of this production, directed by Trevor Nunn and Christopher Hunt, premieres on SKY-TV; it later wins an International Emmy Award.

- November 2003—The NT (formerly RNT) film version of *Oklahoma!* is broadcast on PBS' *Great Performances* and released on DVD by Image Entertainment.

February 23, 2002—Previews begin at the Gershwin Theatre on Broadway for the Cameron Mackintosh production of the NT staging of *Oklahoma!*, directed by Trevor Nunn and choreographed by Susan Stroman, with a cast headed by Patrick Wilson (Curly), Andrea Martin (Aunt Eller), and, recreating their London roles, Josefina Gabrielle and Shuler Hensley (who wins a Tony Award for his performance).

- March 21, 2002—This production premieres with a star-studded opening night with an audience including members of the original Broadway cast (such as Joan Roberts and Celeste Holm), Shirley Jones from the film version, and a delegation of Oklahomans lead by their governor, Frank Keating.

- June 28, 2002—On the occasion of its composer Richard Rodgers' one hundredth birthday, the company of *Oklahoma!* hosts a concert tribute on their stage, free and open to the public.

- February 23, 2003—After a full year on Broadway, *Oklahoma!* closes to prepare for a U.S. national tour.

- December 16, 2003—The U.S. national tour begins in Denver, Colorado, and plays in more than two dozen American cities over the next two years.

Winter 2004—The Oklahoma State Department of Public Safety announces that every driver's license issued in the state will feature the lyric "We know we belong to the land/And the land we belong to is grand!" from "Oklahoma." With a four-year cycle of renewal, the state ensures that the R&H lyric sits in the pocket of every licensed Oklahoma driver—over 4 million strong—in time for the state's centennial.

2006–7—To commemorate the centennial of the state of Oklahoma (which joined the Union in November 1907), the Rodgers & Hammerstein Organization joins forces with the Oklahoma Centennial Commission to oversee more than a year of celebrations beginning in November 2006. Among its highlights are:

- The world premiere of *Oklahoma! Suite*, a ballet created by Tulsa Ballet and based on Agnes de Mille's landmark dance pieces from the musical.

- On Thanksgiving Day 2006, Oklahoma native Kristin Chenoweth rides an Oklahoma state float in the Macy's

Thanksgiving Day Parade and belts out her state's anthem on national television.

- In January 2007, the U.S. Postal Service issues a stamp commemorating the state, featuring the appropriate Hammerstein lyric ("Oh, what a beautiful mornin'") over the image of an Oklahoma sunrise.

- Throughout 2007, Lyric Theatre of Oklahoma brings a special version of the musical to nearly every school in the state through its *Oklahoma!* Interactive program, connecting with over 35,000 Oklahoma students.

To Date—R&H Theatricals licenses more than six hundred productions of *Oklahoma!* annually in the United States and Canada alone. Worldwide, *Oklahoma!* has been translated into over a dozen languages, including French, German, Greek, Italian, Russian, Japanese, Hebrew, Icelandic, Norwegian, Hungarian, Estonian, Dutch, and Polish. English-language productions have been seen in Great Britain, Canada, Australia, New Zealand, Ireland, and South Africa.

Bert Fink
The Rodgers & Hammerstein Organization

OKLAHOMA!

OKLAHOMA! *was first produced by The Theatre Guild on March 31, 1943, at the St. James Theatre, New York City, with the following cast:*

(*In order of appearance*)

Aunt Eller	Betty Garde
Curly	Alfred Drake
Laurey	Joan Roberts
Ike Skidmore	Barry Kelley
Fred	Edwin Clay
Slim	Herbert Rissman
Will Parker	Lee Dixon
Jud Fry	Howard da Silva
Ado Annie Carnes	Celeste Holm
Ali Hakim	Joseph Buloff
Gertie Cummings	Jane Lawrence
Ellen	Katharine Sergava
Kate	Ellen Love
Sylvie	Joan McCracken
Armina	Kate Friedlich
Aggie	Bambi Linn
Andrew Carnes	Ralph Riggs
Cord Elam	Owen Martin
Jess	George Church
Chalmers	Marc Platt
Mike	Paul Shiers
Joe	George Irving
Sam	Hayes Gordon

Directed by Rouben Mamoulian
Dances by Agnes de Mille
Settings by Lemuel Ayers
Costumes by Miles White
Orchestra directed by Joseph Schwartzdorf
Orchestrations by Robert Russell Bennett
Production under the supervision of
Theresa Helburn and Lawrence Langner

SCENES

Act One

Act Two

Time: Just after the turn of the century
Place: Indian Territory (Now Oklahoma)

MUSICAL NUMBERS

ACT ONE

Scene I

"Oh, What a Beautiful Mornin'"	CURLY
"The Surrey with the Fringe on Top"	CURLY, LAUREY, AUNT ELLER
"Kansas City"	WILL, AUNT ELLER AND THE BOYS
"I Cain't Say No"	ADO ANNIE
"Many a New Day"	LAUREY AND THE GIRLS
"It's a Scandal! It's a Outrage!"	ALI HAKIM AND THE BOYS AND GIRLS
"People Will Say We're in Love"	CURLY AND LAUREY

Scene II

"Pore Jud"	CURLY AND JUD
"Lonely Room"	JUD

Scene III

"Out of My Dreams"	LAUREY AND THE GIRLS

ACT TWO

Scene I

"The Farmer and the Cowman"	SUNG BY CARNES, AUNT ELLER, CURLY, WILL, ADO ANNIE, FRED AND ENSEMBLE
"All er Nuthin'"	ADO ANNIE AND WILL AND TWO DANCING GIRLS

Scene II
Reprise: "People Will Say We're in Love"   CURLY AND LAUREY

Scene III
"Oklahoma"   CURLY, LAUREY, AUNT ELLER, IKE, FRED
AND ENSEMBLE
Reprise: "Oh, What a Beautiful Mornin'"   LAUREY, CURLY
AND ENSEMBLE
Finale   ENTIRE COMPANY

ACT ONE

Scene I

SCENE: *The front of* LAUREY'S *farmhouse.*

"It is a radiant summer morning several years ago, the kind of morning which, enveloping the shapes of earth men, cattle in a meadow, blades of the young corn, streams—makes them seem to exist now for the first time, their images giving off a golden emanation that is partly true and partly a trick of the imagination, focusing to keep alive a loveliness that may pass away."

AUNT ELLER MURPHY, *a buxom hearty woman about fifty, is seated behind a wooden, brass-banded churn, looking out over the meadow (which is the audience), a contented look on her face. Like the voice of the morning, a song comes from somewhere, growing louder as the young singer comes nearer.*

CURLY (*Off stage*)
    There's a bright, golden haze on the meadow,
    There's a bright, golden haze on the meadow.
    The corn is as high as a elephant's eye
    An' it looks like it's climbin' clear up to the sky.
      (CURLY *saunters on and stands tentatively outside the gate to the front yard*)
    Oh, what a beautiful mornin',
    Oh, what a beautiful day.
    I got a beautiful feelin'
    Ev'rythin's goin' my way.
      (CURLY *opens the gate and walks over to the porch, obviously singing for the benefit of someone inside the house.* AUNT ELLER *looks straight ahead, elaborately ignoring* CURLY)

All the cattle are standin' like statues,
All the cattle are standin' like statues.
They don't turn their heads as they see me ride by,
But a little brown mav'rick is winkin' her eye.
Oh, what a beautiful mornin',
Oh, what a beautiful day.
I got a beautiful feelin'
Ev'rythin's goin' my way.
(CURLY *comes up behind* AUNT ELLER *and shouts in her ear*)
Hi, Aunt Eller!

AUNT ELLER   Skeer me to death! Whut're you doin' around here?

CURLY   Come a-singin' to you.
    (*Strolling a few steps away*)
All the sounds of the earth are like music—
All the sounds of the earth are like music.
The breeze is so busy it don't miss a tree
And a ol' weepin' willer is laughin' at me!
Oh, what a beautiful mornin',
Oh, what a beautiful day.
I got a beautiful feelin'
Ev'rythin's goin' my way....
Oh, what a beautiful day!
    (AUNT ELLER *resumes churning.* CURLY *looks wistfully up at the windows of the house, then turns back to* AUNT ELLER)

AUNT ELLER   If I wasn't a ole womern, and if you wasn't so young and smart-alecky—why, I'd marry you and git you to set around at night and sing to me.

CURLY   No, you wouldn't neither. Cuz I wouldn't marry you ner none of yer kinfolks, I could he'p it.

AUNT ELLER (*Wisely*)   Oh, none of my kinfolks, huh?

CURLY (*Raising his voice so that laurey will hear if she is inside the house*)   And you c'n tell 'em that, *all* of 'm includin' that niece of your'n, Miss Laurey Williams! (AUNT ELLER *continues to churn.* CURLY *comes down to her and speaks deliberately*) Aunt Eller, if you was to tell me whur Laurey was at—whur would you tell me she was at?

AUNT ELLER   I wouldn't tell you a-tall. Fer as fer as I c'n make out, Laurey ain't payin' you no heed.

CURLY   So, she don't take to me much, huh? Whur'd you git sich a uppity niece 'at wouldn't pay no heed to me? Who's the best bronc buster in this yere territory?

AUNT ELLER   You, I bet.

CURLY   And the best bull-dogger in seventeen counties? Me, that's who! And looky here, I'm handsome, ain't I?

AUNT ELLER   Purty as a pitcher.

CURLY   Curly-headed, ain't I? And bow-legged from the saddle fer God knows how long, ain't I?

AUNT ELLER   Couldn't stop a pig in the road.

CURLY   Well, whut else does she want then, the damn she-mule?

AUNT ELLER   I don't know. But I'm shore sartin it ain't you. Who you takin' to the Box Social tonight?

CURLY   Ain't thought much about it.

AUNT ELLER   Bet you come over to ast Laurey.

CURLY   Whut 'f I did?

AUNT ELLER   You astin' me too? I'll wear my fascinator.

CURLY   Yeow, you too.

LAUREY (*Singing off stage*)
  Oh, what a beautiful mornin'
  (*She enters*)
  Oh, what a beautiful day
  (*Spoken as she gives* CURLY *a brief glance*)
  Oh, I thought you was somebody.
  (*She resumes singing, crosses to clothesline and hangs up an apron*)
  I got a beautiful feelin'
  Ev'rythin's goin' my way.
  (*Spoken as she comes down to* AUNT ELLER)
  Is this all that's come-a-callin' and it a'ready ten o'clock of a Sattiddy mornin'?

CURLY   You knowed it was me 'fore you opened the door.

LAUREY   No sich of a thing.

CURLY   You did, too! You heared my voice and knowed it was me.

LAUREY   I heared a voice a-talkin' rumbly along with Aunt Eller. And heared someone a-singin' like a bullfrog in a pond.

CURLY   You knowed it was me, so you set in there a-thinkin' up sump'n mean to say. I'm a good mind not to ast you to the Box Social.
(AUNT ELLER *rises, crosses to clothesline, takes down quilt, folds it, puts it on porch*)

LAUREY   If you did ast me, I wouldn't go with you. Besides, how'd you take me? You ain't bought a new buggy with red wheels onto it, have you?

CURLY   No, I ain't.

LAUREY   And a spankin' team with their bridles all jinglin'?

CURLY   No.

LAUREY   'Spect me to ride on behind ole Dun, I guess. You better ast that ole Cummin's girl you've tuck sich a shine to, over acrost the river.

CURLY   If I was to ast you, they'd be a way to take you, Miss Laurey Smarty.

LAUREY   Oh, they would?
(CURLY *now proceeds to stagger* LAUREY *with an idea. But she doesn't let on at first how she is "tuck up" with it.* AUNT ELLER *is the one who falls like a ton of bricks immediately and helps* CURLY *try to sell it to* LAUREY.)

CURLY

When I take you out tonight with me,
Honey, here's the way it's goin' to be;
You will set behind a team of snow-white horses
In the slickest gig you ever see!

AUNT ELLER   Lands!

CURLY

Chicks and ducks and geese better scurry
When I take you out in the surrey,
When I take you out in the surrey with the fringe on top!
Watch thet fringe and see how it flutters
When I drive them high-steppin' strutters!
Nosey-pokes'll peek through their shutters and their eyes will
    pop!
The wheels are yeller, the upholstery's brown,
The dashboard's genuine leather,
With isinglass curtains y'c'n roll right down
In case there's a change in the weather—
Two bright side-lights, winkin' and blinkin',
Ain't no finer rig, I'm a-thinkin'!
You c'n keep yer rig if you're thinkin' 'at I'd keer to swap
Fer that shiny little surrey with the fringe on the top!
    (LAUREY *still pretends unconcern, but she is obviously slipping*)

AUNT ELLER   Would y'say the fringe was made of silk?

CURLY   Wouldn't have no other kind but silk.

LAUREY (*She's only human*)   Has it really got a team of snow-
white horses?

CURLY One's like snow—the other's more like milk.

AUNT ELLER So y'can tell 'em apart!

CURLY

All the world'll fly in a flurry
When I take you out in the surrey,
When I take you out in the surrey with the fringe on top!
When we hit that road, hell fer leather,
Cats and dogs'll dance in the heather,
Birds and frogs'll sing all together and the toads will hop!
The wind'll whistle as we rattle along,
The cows'll moo in the clover,
The river will ripple out a whispered song,
And whisper it over and over:
   (*In a loud whisper*)
Don't you wisht y'd go on ferever?
Don't you wisht y'd go on ferever?
   (AUNT ELLER's *and* LAUREY's *lips move involuntarily, shaping*
   the same words)
Don't you wisht y'd go on ferever and ud never stop
In that shiny little surrey with the fringe on the top?
   (*Music continues under dialogue*)

AUNT ELLER Y'd shore feel like a queen settin' up in *that* carriage!

CURLY (*Over-confident*) On'y she talked so mean to me a while
back, Aunt Eller, I'm a good mind not to take her.

LAUREY Ain't said I was goin'!

CURLY (*The fool*) Ain't ast you!

LAUREY   Whur'd you git sich a rig at? (*With explosive laughter,
seeing a chance for revenge*) Anh! I bet he's went and h'ard a rig
over to Claremore! Thinkin' I'd go with him!

CURLY   'S all you know about it.

LAUREY   Spent all his money h'arin' a rig and now ain't got nobody to ride in it!

CURLY   Have, too! . . . Did not h'ar it. Made the whole thing
up outa my head.

LAUREY   What! Made it up?

CURLY   Dashboard and all.

LAUREY (*Flying at him*)   Oh! Git offa the place, you! Aunt Eller,
make him git hisse'f outa here. (*She picks up a fly swatter and
chases him*) Tellin' me lies!

CURLY (*Dodging her*)   Makin' up a few—look out now! (*He jumps
the fence to save himself.* LAUREY *turns her back to him, and sits
down. He comes up behind her. The music, which had become
more turbulent to match the scene, now softens*) Makin' up a few
purties ain't agin' no law 'at I know of. Don't you wisht they
was such a rig, though? (*Winking at* AUNT ELLER) Nen y'could
go to the play party and do a hoe-down till mornin' if you was
a mind to. . . . Nen when you was all wore out, I'd lift you onto
the surrey, and jump up alongside of you—And we'd jist point
the horses home. . . . I can jist pitcher the whole thing. (AUNT
ELLER *beams on them as* CURLY *sings very softly:*)

I can see the stars gittin' blurry
When we ride back home in the surrey,
Ridin' slowly home in the surrey with the fringe on top.
I can feel the day gittin' older,
Feel a sleepy head near my shoulder,
Noddin', droopin' close to my shoulder till it falls, kerplop!
The sun is swimmin' on the rim of a hill,
The moon is takin' a header,
And jist as I'm thinkin' all the earth is still,
A lark'll wake up in the medder. . . .
Hush! You bird, my baby's a-sleepin'—
Maybe got a dream worth a-keepin'
    (*Soothing and slower*)
Whoa! You team, and jist keep a-creepin' at a slow clip-clop.
Don't you hurry with the surrey with the fringe on the top.
    (*There is a silence and contentment, but only for a brief moment.* LAUREY *starts slowly to emerge from the enchantment of his description*)

LAUREY   On'y . . . on'y there ain't no sich rig. You said you made the whole thing up.

CURLY   Well . . .

LAUREY   Why'd you come around here with yer stories and lies, gittin' me all worked up that-a-way? Talkin' 'bout the sun swimmin' on the hill, and all—like it was so. Who'd want to ride 'longside of you anyway?
    (IKE *and* FRED *enter and stand outside the gate, looking on.*)

AUNT ELLER   Whyn't you jist grab her and kiss her when she acts that-a-way, Curly? She's jist achin' fer you to, I bet.

LAUREY   Oh, I won't even speak to him, let alone 'low him to kiss me, the braggin', bow-legged, wisht-he-had-a-sweetheart bum! (*She flounces into the house, slamming the door.*)

AUNT ELLER   She likes you—quite a lot.

CURLY   Whew! If she liked me any more she'd sic the dogs onto me.

IKE   Y'git the wagon hitched up?

AUNT ELLER   Whut wagon?

CURLY   They's a crowd of folks comin' down from Bushyhead for the Box Social.

FRED   Curly said mebbe you'd loan us yer big wagon to bring 'em up from the station.

AUNT ELLER   Course I would, if he'd ast me.

CURLY (*Embarrassed*)   Got to talkin' 'bout a lot of other things. I'll go hitch up the horses now 'f you say it's all right.
(*As he exits, a group of boys run on, leaping the fence, shouting boisterously and pushing* WILL PARKER *in front of them.* WILL *is apparently a favorite with* AUNT ELLER.)

SLIM   See whut we brung you, Aunt Eller!

AUNT ELLER   Hi, Will!

WILL   Hi, Aunt Eller!

AUNT ELLER   Whut happened up at the fair? You do any good in the steer ropin'?

WILL   I did purty good. I won it. (*The following three speeches overlap.*)

IKE   Good boy!

FRED   Always knowed y'would.

AUNT ELLER   Ain't nobody c'n sling a rope like our territory boys.

WILL   Cain't stay but a minnit, Aunt Eller. Got to git over to Ado Annie. Don't you remember, her paw said 'f I ever was worth fifty dollars I could have her?

AUNT ELLER   Fifty dollars! That whut they give you fer prize money?

WILL   That's whut!

AUNT ELLER   Lands, if Ado Annie's paw keeps his promise we'll be dancin' at yer weddin'.

WILL   If he don't keep his promise I'll take her right from under his nose, and I won't give him the present I brung fer him. (*He takes "The Little Wonder" from his pocket. This is a small cylindrical toy with a peep-hole at one end*) Look, fellers, whut I got for Ado Annie's paw! (*The boys crowd around*) 'Scuse us, Aunt Eller. (*Illustrating to the boys, lowering his voice*) You hold it up to yer eyes, like this. Then when you git a good look, you turn it around at th' top and the pitcher changes.

IKE (*Looking into it*)   Well, I'll be side-gaited!
(*The boys line up, and take turns, making appropriate exclamations.*)

WILL   They call it "The Little Wonder"!

AUNT ELLER   Silly goats! (*But her curiosity gets the better of her. She yanks a little man out of the line, takes his place, gets hold of "The Little Wonder" and takes a look*) The hussy! . . . Ought to be ashamed of herself. (*Glaring at* WILL) You, too! . . . How do you turn the thing to see the other pitcher? (*Looking again, and turning*) Wait, I'm gettin' it. . . . (*When she gets it, she takes it away from her eye quickly and, handing it to* WILL, *walks away in shocked silence. Then she suddenly "busts out laughin'"*) I'm a good mind to tell Ado Annie on yer.

WILL   Please don't, Aunt Eller. She wouldn't understand.

AUNT ELLER   No tellin' what you been up to. Bet you carried on plenty in Kansas City.

WILL   I wouldn't call it carryin' on. But I shore did see some things I never see before. (*Sings*)
I got to Kansas City on a Frid'y.
By Sattidy I l'arned a thing or two.
For up to then I didn't have an idy
Of whut the modren world was comin' to!
I counted twenty gas buggies goin' by theirsel's

Almost ev'ry time I tuck a walk.
Nen I put my ear to a Bell Telephone
And a strange womern started in to talk!

AUNT ELLER   Whut next!

BOYS   Yeah, whut!

WILL   Whut next?
Ev'rythin's up to date in Kansas City.
They've gone about as fur as they c'n go!
They went and built a skyscraper seven stories high—
About as high as a buildin' orta grow.
Ev'rythin's like a dream in Kansas City.
It's better than a magic-lantern show!
Y' c'n turn the radiator on whenever you want some heat.
With ev'ry kind o' comfort ev'ry house is all complete.
You c'n walk to privies in the rain an' never wet yer feet!
They've gone about as fur as they c'n go!

ALL
Yes, sir!
They've gone about as fur as they c'n go!

WILL
Ev'rythin's up to date in Kansas City.
They've gone about as fur as they c'n go!
They got a big theayter they call a burleeque.
Fer fifty cents you c'n see a dandy show.
One of the gals was fat and pink and pretty,
As round above as she was round below.

I could swear that she was padded from her shoulder to her
  heel,
But later in the second act when she begun to peel
She proved that ev'rythin' she had was absolutely real!
She went about as fur as she could go!

ALL

Yes, sir!
She went about as fur as she could go!
  (WILL *starts two-stepping.*)

IKE   Whut you doin'?

WILL   This is the two-step. That's all they're dancin' nowadays.
The waltz is through. Ketch on to it? A one and a two—a
one and a two. Course they don't do it alone. C'mon, Aunt
Eller.
  (WILL *dances* AUNT ELLER *around. At the end of the refrain
  she is all tuckered out.*)

AUNT ELLER   And that's about as fur as I c'n go!

ALL

Yes, sir!
And that's about as fur as she c'n go!
  (WILL *starts to dance alone.*)

FRED   Whut you doin' now, Will?

WILL   That's rag-time. Seen a couple of fellers doin' it.
  (*And* WILL *does his stuff, accompanied by four of the dancing
  boys. At the end of the number* CURLY *enters.*)

CURLY   Team's all hitched.

WILL   'Lo, Curly. Cain't stop to talk. Goin' over to Ado Annie's. I got fifty dollars.

IKE   Time we got goin', boys. Thanks fer the loan of the wagon, Aunt Eller. (*They all start to leave*) Come on, Curly.

CURLY   I'll ketch up with you. (*He makes sure* IKE *is well on his way, then turns to* AUNT ELLER) Aunt Eller, I got to know sumpin'. Listen, who's the low, filthy sneak 'at Laurey's got her cap set for?

AUNT ELLER   You.

CURLY   Never mind 'at. They must be plenty of men a-tryin' to spark her. And she shorely leans to one of 'em. Now don't she?

AUNT ELLER   Well, they is that fine farmer, Jace Hutchins, jist this side of Lone Ellum— Nen thet ole widder man at Claremore, makes out he's a doctor or a vet'nary—
    (JUD, *a burly, scowling man enters, carrying firewood.*)

CURLY   That's whut I thought. Hello, Jud.

JUD   Hello, yourself.
    (JUD *exits into house.*)

AUNT ELLER (*Significantly, looking in* JUD'*s direction*)   Nen of course there's someone nearer home that's got her on his mind most of the time, till he don't know a plow from a thrashin' machine.

CURLY (*Jerking his head up toward the house*)   Him?

AUNT ELLER   Yeah, Jud Fry.

CURLY   That bullet-colored, growly man?

AUNT ELLER   Now don't you go and say nuthin' agin' him! He's the best hired hand I ever had. Jist about runs the farm by hisself. Well, two women couldn't do it, you orta know that.

CURLY   Laurey'd take up 'th a man like that!

AUNT ELLER   I ain't said she's tuck up with him.

CURLY   Well, he's around all the time, ain't he? Lives here.

AUNT ELLER   Out in the smokehouse.
   (JUD *and* LAUREY *enter from the house.* JUD *crosses and speaks to* AUNT ELLER)

JUD   Changed my mind about cleanin' the henhouse today. Leavin' it till tomorrow. Got to quit early cuz I'm drivin' Laurey over to the party tonight.
   (*A bombshell!*)

CURLY   You're drivin' Laurey?

JUD   Ast her.
   (*Pointing to* LAUREY, *who doesn't deny it.* JUD *exits.* CURLY *is completely deflated.*)

CURLY   Well, wouldn't that just make you bawl! Well, don't fergit,

Aunt Eller. You and me's got a date together. And if you make up a nice box of lunch, mebbe I'll bid fer it.

AUNT ELLER   How we goin', Curly? In that rig you made up? I'll ride a-straddle of them lights a-winkin' like lightnin' bugs!

CURLY   That there ain't no made-up rig, you hear me? I h'ard it over to Claremore.
(*This stuns* LAUREY.)

AUNT ELLER   Lands, you did?

CURLY   Shore did. (*Refrain of the "Surrey Song" starts in orchestra*) Purty one, too. When I come callin' fer you right after supper, see that you got yer beauty spots fastened onto you proper, so you won't lose 'em off, you hear? 'At's a right smart turnout.
(*His voice, a little husky, picks up the refrain:*)
    The wheels are yeller, the upholstery's brown,
    The dashboard's genuine leather,
    With isinglass curtains y'c'n roll right down,
    In case there's a change in the weather—
    (*He breaks off in the song*)
See you before tonight anyways, on the way back from the station—
    (*Turning, singing to himself as he saunters off:*)
    Ain't no finer rig, I'm a-thinkin' . . . 'at I'd keer to swap
    Fer that shiny little surrey with the fringe on the top—
    (*He is off.*)

AUNT ELLER (*Calling off the stage to him*)   Hey, Curly, tell all the girls in Bushyhead to stop by here and freshen up. It's a long way to Skidmore's. (*Maybe* LAUREY *would like to "bust out" into tears, but she bites her lip, and doesn't.* AUNT ELLER *studies her for a moment after* CURLY *has gone, then starts up toward the house*) That means we'll have a lot of company. Better pack yer lunch hamper.

LAUREY (*A strange, sudden panic in her voice*)   Aunt Eller, don't go to Skidmore's with Curly tonight. If you do, I'll have to ride with Jud all alone.

AUNT ELLER   That's the way you wanted it, ain't it?

LAUREY   No. I did it because Curly was so fresh. But I'm afraid to tell Jud I won't go, Aunt Eller. He'd do sumpin turrible. He makes me shivver ever' time he gits clost to me. . . . Ever go down to that ole smokehouse where he's at?

AUNT ELLER   Plen'y times. Why?

LAUREY   Did you see them pitchers he's got tacked onto the walls?

AUNT ELLER   Oh, yeah, I seed them. But don't you pay them no mind.

LAUREY   Sumpin' wrong inside him, Aunt Eller. I hook my door at night and fasten my winders agin' it. Agin' *it*—and the sound of feet a-walkin' up and down out there under that tree outside my room.

AUNT ELLER   Laurey!

LAUREY   Mornin's he comes to his breakfast and looks at me

out from under his eyebrows like sumpin back in the bresh som'eres. I know whut I'm talkin' about.
(*Voices off stage. It's* ADO ANNIE *and the* PEDDLER.)

AUNT ELLER   You crazy young 'un! Stop actin' like a chicken with its head cut off! Now who'd you reckon that is drove up? Why, it's that ole peddler! The one that sold me that egg-beater!

LAUREY (*Looking off*)   He's got Ado Annie with him! Will Parker's Ado Annie!

AUNT ELLER   Ole peddler! You know whut he tol' me? Tol' me that egg-beater ud beat up eggs, and wring out dishrags, and turn the ice-cream freezer, and I don't know whut all!

LAUREY (*Calling off stage*)   Yoohoo! Ado Annie!

AUNT ELLER (*Shouting off stage*)   Hold yer horses, Peddler-man! I want to talk to you!
(*She starts off, as* ADO ANNIE *enters with lunch hamper.*)

ADO ANNIE   Hi, Aunt Eller!

AUNT ELLER   Hi, yourself.
(AUNT ELLER *exits.*)

ADO ANNIE   Hello, Laurey.

LAUREY   Hello. Will Parker's back from Kansas City. He's lookin' fer yer.
(ADO ANNIE's *brows knit to meet a sudden problem.*)

ADO ANNIE   Will Parker! I didn't count on him bein' back so soon!

LAUREY   I can see that! Been ridin' a piece?

ADO ANNIE   The peddler-man's gonna drive me to the Box Social. I got up sort of a tasty lunch.

LAUREY   Ado Annie! Have you tuck up with that peddler-man?

ADO ANNIE   N-not yit.

LAUREY   But yer promised to Will Parker, ain't yer?

ADO ANNIE   Not what you might say *promised*. I jist told him mebbe.

LAUREY   Don't y' like him no more?

ADO ANNIE   'Course I do. They won't never be nobody like Will.

LAUREY   Then whut about this peddler-man?

ADO ANNIE (*Looking off wistfully*)   They won't never be nobody like *him*, neither.

LAUREY   Well, which one d'you like the best?

ADO ANNIE   Whutever one I'm with!

LAUREY   Well, you air a silly!

ADO ANNIE   Now, Laurey, you know they didn't nobody pay me
no mind up to this year, count of I was scrawny and flat as a
beanpole. 'Nen I kind of rounded up a little and now the boys
act diff'rent to me.

LAUREY   Well, whut's wrong with that?

ADO ANNIE   Nuthin' wrong. I like it. I like it so much when
a feller talks purty to me I git all shaky from horn to hoof!
Don't you?

LAUREY   Cain't think whut yer talkin' about.

ADO ANNIE   Don't you feel kind of sorry fer a feller when he
looks like he wants to kiss you?

LAUREY   Well, you jist cain't go around kissin' every man that
asts you! Didn't anybody ever tell you that?

ADO ANNIE   Yeow, they *told* me. . . . (*Sings*)
    It ain't so much a question of not knowin' whut to do,
    I knowed whut's right and wrong since I been ten.
    I heared a lot of stories—and I reckon they are true—
    About how girls're put upon by men.
    I know I mustn't fall into the pit,
    But when I'm with a feller—I fergit!
    I'm jist a girl who cain't say no,
    I'm in a terrible fix
    I always say, come on, le's go—
    Jist when I orta say nix!

When a person tries to kiss a girl
I know she orta give his face a smack.
But as soon as someone kisses me
I somehow sorta wanta kiss him back!
I'm jist a fool when lights are low.
I cain't be prissy and quaint—
I ain't the type thet c'n faint—
How c'n I be whut I ain't?
I cain't say no!

Whut you goin' to do when a feller gits flirty
And starts to talk purty?
Whut you goin' to do?
S'posin' 'at he says 'at yer lips're like cherries,
Er roses, er berries?
Whut you goin' to do?
S'posin' 'at he says 'at you're sweeter'n cream
And he's gotta have cream er die?
Whut you goin' to do when he talks thet way?
Spit in his eye?

I'm jist a girl who cain't say no,
Cain't seem to say it at all.
I hate to disserpoint a beau
When he is payin' a call.
Fer a while I ack refined and cool,
A-settin' on the velveteen settee—
Nen I think of thet ol' golden rule,
And do fer him whut he would do fer me!
I cain't resist a Romeo
In a sombrero and chaps.
Soon as I sit on their laps

Somethin' inside of me snaps
I cain't say no!
(*She sits on her hamper, and looks discouraged*)

I'm jist a girl who cain't say no.
Kissin's my favorite food.
With er without the mistletoe
I'm in a holiday mood!
Other girls are coy and hard to catch
But other girls ain't havin' any fun!
Ev'ry time I lose a wrestlin' match
I have a funny feelin' that I won!
Though I c'n feel the undertow,
I never make a complaint
Till it's too late fer restraint,
Then when I want to I cain't.
I cain't say no!
(*Resuming dialogue, after applause*)
It's like I tole you, I git sorry fer them!

LAUREY   I wouldn't feel sorry fer any man, no matter whut!

ADO ANNIE   I'm shore sorry fer pore Ali Hakim now. Look how Aunt Eller's cussin' him out!

LAUREY   Ali Hakim! That his name?

ADO ANNIE   Yeah, it's Persian.

LAUREY   You shore fer sartin you love him better'n you love Will?

ADO ANNIE   I *was* shore. And now that ole Will has to come home and first thing you know he'll start talkin' purty to me and changin' my mind back!

LAUREY   But Will wants to marry you.

ADO ANNIE   So does Ali Hakim.

LAUREY   Did he ast yer?

ADO ANNIE   Not direckly. But how I know is he said this mornin' that he wanted fer me to drive like that with him to the end of the world. Well, 'f we drove only as fur as Catoosie that'd take to sundown, wouldn't it? Nen we'd have to go som'eres and be all night together, and bein' together all night means he wants a weddin', don't it?

LAUREY   Not to a peddler it don't!
     (*Enter* PEDDLER *and* AUNT ELLER.)

PEDDLER   All right! All right! If the egg-beater don't work I give you something just as good!

AUNT ELLER   Jist as good! It's got to be a thousand million times better!
     (*The* PEDDLER *puts down his bulging suitcase, his little beady eyes sparkling professionally. He rushes over and, to* LAUREY'*s alarm, kisses her hand.*)

PEDDLER   My, oh, my! Miss Laurey! Jippity crickets, how high you have growed up! Last time I come through here, you was tiny like a shrimp, with freckles. Now look at you—a great big beautiful lady!

LAUREY   Quit it a-bitin' me! If you ain't had no breakfast go and eat yerself a green apple.

PEDDLER   Now, Aunt Eller, just lissen—

AUNT ELLER (*Shouting*)   I ain't yer Aunt Eller! Don't you call me Aunt Eller, you little wart. I'm mad at you.

PEDDLER   Don't you go and be mad at me. Ain't I said I'd give you a present? (*Getting his bag*) Something to wear.

AUNT ELLER   Foot! Got things fer to wear. Wouldn't have it. Whut is it?

PEDDLER (*Holding up garter*)   Real silk. Made in Persia!

AUNT ELLER   Whut'd I want with a ole Persian garter?

ADO ANNIE   They look awful purty, Aunt Eller, with bows onto 'em and all.

AUNT ELLER   I'll try 'em on.

PEDDLER   Hold out your foot.
   (AUNT ELLER *obeys mechanically. But when he gets the garter over her ankle, she kicks him down.*)

AUNT ELLER   Did you have any idy I was goin' ter let you slide that garter up my limb? (*She stoops over and starts to pull the garter up*) Grab onto my petticoats, Laurey.
   (*Noticing the* PEDDLER *looking at her, she turns her back on him pointedly and goes on with the operation. The* PEDDLER *turns to* ADO ANNIE.)

PEDDLER   Funny woman. Would be much worse if I tried to take your garters off.

ADO ANNIE   Yeh, cuz that ud make her stockin's fall down, wouldn't it?

AUNT ELLER   Now give me the other one.

PEDDLER   Which one? (*Picking it out of his case*) Oh, you want to buy this one to match?

AUNT ELLER   Whut do you mean do I want to *buy* it?

PEDDLER   I can let you have it for fifty cents—four bits.

AUNT ELLER   Do you want me to get that egg-beater and ram it down yer windpipe!
(*She snatches the second one away.*)

PEDDLER   All right—all right. Don't anybody want to buy something? How about you, Miss Laurey? Must be wanting something—a pretty young girl like you.

LAUREY   Me? Course I want sumpin. (*Working up to a kind of abstracted ecstasy*) Want a buckle made outa shiny silver to fasten onto my shoes! Want a dress with lace. Want perfume, wanta be purty, wanta smell like a honeysuckle vine!

AUNT ELLER   Give her a cake of soap.

LAUREY   Want things I've heared of and never had before— a rubber-t'ard buggy, a cut-glass sugar bowl. Want things I cain't tell you about—not only things to look at and hold in yer hands. Things to happen to you. Things so nice, if they ever did happen to you, yer heart ud quit beatin'. You'd fall down dead!

PEDDLER I've got just the thing for you! (*He fishes into his satchel and pulls out a bottle*) The Elixir of Egypt! (*He holds the bottle high.*)

LAUREY What's 'at?

PEDDLER It's a secret formula, belonged to Pharaoh's daughter!

AUNT ELLER (*Leaning over and putting her nose to it*)   Smellin' salts!

PEDDLER (*Snatching it away*)   But a special kind of smelling salts. Read what it says on the label: "Take a deep breath and you see everything clear." That's what Pharaoh's daughter used to do. When she had a hard problem to decide, like what prince she ought to marry, or what dress to wear to a party, or whether she ought to cut off somebody's head—she'd take a whiff of this.

LAUREY (*Excited*)   I'll take a bottle of that, Mr. Peddler.

PEDDLER Precious stuff.

LAUREY How much?

PEDDLER Two bits.
      (*She pays him and takes the bottle.*)

AUNT ELLER   Throwin' away yer money!

LAUREY (*Holding the bottle close to her, thinking aloud*)   Helps you decide what to do!

PEDDLER   Now don't you want me to show you some pretty dewdads? You know, with lace around the bottom, and ribbons running in and out?

AUNT ELLER   You mean fancy drawers?

PEDDLER (*Taking a pair out of pack*)   All made in Paris.

AUNT ELLER   Well, I never wear that kind myself, but I shore do like to look at 'em.
(PEDDLER *takes out a pair of red flannel drawers.*)

ADO ANNIE (*Dubiously*)   Y-yeah, they's all right—if you ain't goin' no place.

AUNT ELLER   Bring yer trappin's inside and mebbe I c'n find you sumpin to eat and drink.
(AUNT ELLER *exits.* PEDDLER *starts to repack. The two girls whisper for a moment.*)

LAUREY   Well, ast him, why don't you?
(*She giggles and exits into house.*)

ADO ANNIE   Ali, Laurey and me've been havin' a argument.

PEDDLER   About what, Baby?

ADO ANNIE   About what you meant when you said that about drivin' with me to the end of the world.

PEDDLER (*Cagily*)   Well, I didn't mean really to the end of the world.

ADO ANNIE   Then how fur did you want to go?

PEDDLER   Oh, about as far as—say—Claremore—to the hotel.

ADO ANNIE   Whut's at the hotel?

PEDDLER (*Ready for the kill*)   In front of the hotel is a veranda— inside is a lobby—upstairs—upstairs might be Paradise.

ADO ANNIE   I thought they was jist bedrooms.

PEDDLER   For you and me, Baby—Paradise.

ADO ANNIE   Y'see! I knew I was right and Laurey was wrong! You do want to marry me, don't you?

PEDDLER (*Embracing her impulsively*)   Ah, Ado Annie! (*Pulling away*) What did you say?

ADO ANNIE   I said you do want to marry me, don't you. What did you say?

PEDDLER   I didn't say nothing!

WILL (*Off stage*)   Whoa, Suzanna! Yoohoo, Ado Annie, I'm back!

ADO ANNIE   Oh, foot! Jist when—'Lo, Will! (WILL *lets out a whoop off stage*) That's Will Parker. Promise me you won't fight him.

PEDDLER   Why fight? I never saw the man before.
(WILL *enters.*)

WILL   Ado Annie! How's my honey-bunch? How's the sweetest little hundred-and-ten pounds of sugar in the territory?

ADO ANNIE (*Confused*)   Er— Will, this is Ali Hakim.

WILL   How are yuh, Hak? Don't mind the way I talk. 'S all right. I'm goin' to marry her.

PEDDLER (*Delighted*)   Marry her? On purpose?

WILL   Well, sure.

ADO ANNIE   No sich of a thing!

PEDDLER   It's a wonderful thing to be married.
(*He starts off.*)

ADO ANNIE   Ali!

PEDDLER   I got a brother in Persia, got six wives.

ADO ANNIE   Six wives? All at once?

WILL   Shore. 'At's a way they do in them countries.

PEDDLER   Not always. I got another brother in Persia only got one wife. He's a bachelor. (*Exit.*)

ADO ANNIE   Look, Will—

WILL   Look, Will, nuthin'. Know whut I got fer first prize at the fair? Fifty dollars!

ADO ANNIE   Well, that was good. . . . (*The significance suddenly dawning on her*) Fifty dollars?

WILL   Ketch on? Yer paw promised I cud marry you 'f I cud git fifty dollars.

ADO ANNIE   'At's right, he did.

WILL   Know whut I done with it? Spent it all on presents fer you!

ADO ANNIE   But if you spent it you ain't got the cash.

WILL   Whut I got is worth more'n the cash. Feller who sold me the stuff told me!

ADO ANNIE   But, Will . . .

WILL   Stop sayin' "But, Will"— When do I git a little kiss? . . . Oh, Ado Annie, honey, y'aint been off my mind since I left. All the time at the fair grounds even, when I was chasin' steers. I'd rope one under the hoofs and pull him up sharp, and he'd land on his little rump . . . Nen I'd think of you.

ADO ANNIE   Don't start talkin' purty, Will.

WILL   See a lot of beautiful gals in Kansas City. Didn't give one a look.

ADO ANNIE   How could you see 'em if you didn't give 'em a look?

WILL   I mean I didn't look lovin' at 'em—like I look at you. (*He turns her around and looks adoring and pathetic.*)

ADO ANNIE (*Backing away*)   Oh, Will, please don't look at me like that! I cain't bear it.

WILL   Won't stop lookin' like this till you give me a little ole kiss.

ADO ANNIE   Oh, whut's a little ole kiss?

WILL   Nothin'—less'n it comes from you. (*Both stop.*)

ADO ANNIE (*Sighing*)   You do talk purty! (WILL *steps up for his kiss. She nearly gives in, but with sudden and unaccounted-for strength of character she turns away*) No, I won't!

WILL (*Singing softly, seductively, "getting" her*)
  S'posin' 'at I say 'at yer lips're like cherries,
  Er roses er berries?
  Whut you gonna do?
    (*Putting her hand on his heart*)
  Cain't you feel my heart palpatin' an' bumpin',

A-waitin' fer sumpin,
Sumpin nice from you?
I gotta git a kiss an' it's gotta be quick
Er I'll jump in a crick an' die!

ADO ANNIE (*Overcome*)   Whut's a girl to say when you talk that-
a-way?

(*And he gets his kiss. The boys and girls, and* CURLY *and* GERTIE
enter with lunch hampers, shouting and laughing. WILL *and*
ADO ANNIE *run off.* AUNT ELLER *and* LAUREY *come out of the*
house. GERTIE *laughs musically.* LAUREY, *unmindful of the*
group of girls she has been speaking to, looks across at CURLY
and GERTIE *and boils over. All the couples and* CURLY *and*
GERTIE *waltz easily, while they sing:*)

ALL
Oh, what a beautiful mornin',

CURLY
Oh, what a beautiful day.

ALL
I got a beautiful feelin'

CURLY
Ev'rythin's goin' my way. . . .

AUNT ELLER (*To the rescue*)   Hey, Curly! Better take the wagon
down to the troft and give the team some water.

CURLY   Right away, Aunt Eller.
(*He turns.*)

GERTIE   C'n I come, too? Jist love to watch the way you handle horses.

CURLY (*Looking across at* LAUREY)   'At's about all I *can* handle, I guess.

GERTIE   Oh, I cain't believe that, Curly—not from whut I heared about you!
(*She takes his arm and walks him off, turning on more musical laughter. A girl imitates her laugh. Crowd laughs.* LAUREY *takes an involuntary step forward, then stops, frustrated, furious.*)

GIRL   Looks like Curly's tuck up with that Cummin's girl.

LAUREY   Whut'd I keer about that?
(*The girls and* LAUREY *chatter and argue, ad lib.*)

AUNT ELLER   Come on, boys, better git these hampers out under the trees where it's cool.
(*Exit* AUNT ELLER *and boys. To show "how little she keers,"* LAUREY *sings the following song:*)

LAUREY
Why should a woman who is healthy and strong
Blubber like a baby if her man goes away?
A-weepin' and a-wailin' how he's done her wrong—
That's one thing you'll never hear me say!
Never gonna think that the man I lose
Is the only man among men.
I'll snap my fingers to show I don't care.
I'll buy me a brand-new dress to wear.
I'll scrub my neck and I'll bresh my hair,

And start all over again.

Many a new face will please my eye,
Many a new love will find me.
Never've I once looked back to sigh
Over the romance behind me.
Many a new day will dawn before I do!
Many a light lad may kiss and fly,
A kiss gone by is bygone,
Never've I asked an August sky,
"Where has last July gone?"
Never've I wandered through the rye,
Wonderin' where has some guy gone—
Many a new day will dawn before I do!

CHORUS
Many a new face will please my eye,
Many a new love will find me.
Never've I once looked back to sigh
Over the romance behind me.
Many a new day will dawn before I do!

LAUREY
Never've I chased the honey-bee
Who carelessly cajoled me.
Somebody else just as sweet as he
Cheered me and consoled me.
Never've I wept into my tea
Over the deal someone doled me.

CHORUS
Many a new day will dawn,

LAUREY
Many a red sun will set,
Many a blue moon will shine, before I do!
(*A dance follows.* LAUREY *and the girls exit.* PEDDLER *enters from house,* ADO ANNIE *from the other side of the stage.*)

ADO ANNIE   Ali Hakim—

PEDDLER   Hello, kiddo.

ADO ANNIE   I'm shore sorry to see you so happy, cuz whut I got to say will make you mis'able. . . . I got to marry Will.

PEDDLER   That's sad news for me. Well, he is a fine fellow.

ADO ANNIE   Don't hide your feelin's, Ali. I cain't stand it. I'd ruther have you come right out and say yer heart is busted in two.

PEDDLER   Are you positive you got to marry Will?

ADO ANNIE   Shore's shootin'.

PEDDLER   And there is no chance for you to change your mind?

ADO ANNIE   No chance.

PEDDLER (*As if granting a small favor*)   All right, then, my heart is busted in two.

ADO ANNIE   Oh, Ali, you do make up purty things to say!

CARNES (*Off stage*)   That you, Annie?

ADO ANNIE   Hello, Paw. (CARNES *enters. He is a scrappy little man, carrying a shotgun*) Whut you been shootin'?

CARNES   Rabbits. That true whut I hear about Will Parker gittin' fifty dollars?

ADO ANNIE   That's right, Paw. And he wants to hold you to yer promise.

CARNES   Too bad. Still and all I cain't go back on my word.

ADO ANNIE   See, Ali Hakim!

CARNES   I advise you to git that money off'n him before he loses it all. Put it in yer stockin' er inside yer corset where he cain't git at it . . . or can he?

ADO ANNIE   But, Paw—he ain't exackly kep' it. He spent it all on presents . . .
    (*The* PEDDLER *is in a panic.*)

CARNES   See! Whut'd I tell you! Now he cain't have you. I said it had to be fifty dollars cash.

PEDDLER   But, Mr. Carnes, is that fair?

CARNES   Who the hell are you?

ADO ANNIE   This is Ali Hakim.

CARNES   Well, shet your face, er I'll fill yer behind so full of buck-shot, you'll be walkin' around like a duck the rest of yer life.

ADO ANNIE   Ali, if I don't have to marry Will, mebbe your heart don't have to be busted in two like you said.

PEDDLER   I did not say that.

ADO ANNIE   Oh, yes, you did.

PEDDLER   No, I did not.

CARNES   (*Brandishing his gun*)   Are you tryin' to make out my daughter to be a liar?

PEDDLER   No, I'm just making it clear what a liar I am if she's telling the truth.

CARNES   Whut else you been sayin' to my daughter?

ADO ANNIE   (*Before the* PEDDLER *can open his mouth*)   Oh, a awful lot.

CARNES   (*To* PEDDLER)   When?

ADO ANNIE   Las' night, in the moonlight.

CARNES   (*To* PEDDLER)   Where?

ADO ANNIE   'Longside a haystack.

PEDDLER   Listen, Mr. Carnes . . .

CARNES   I'm lissening. Whut else did you say?

ADO ANNIE   He called me his Persian kitten.

CARNES   Why'd you call her that?

PEDDLER   I don't remember.

ADO ANNIE   I do. He said I was like a Persian kitten, cuz they was the cats with the soft round tails.

CARNES (*Cocking his gun*)   That's enough. In this part of the country that better be a proposal of marriage.

ADO ANNIE   That's whut I thought.

CARNES (*To* PEDDLER)   Is that whut you think?

PEDDLER   Look, Mr. Carnes . . .

CARNES (*Taking aim*)   I'm lookin'.

PEDDLER   I'm no good. I'm a peddler. A peddler travels up and down and all around and you'd hardly ever see your daughter no more.

CARNES (*Patting him on back*)   That'd be all right. Take keer of her, son. Take keer of my little rosebud.

ADO ANNIE   Oh, Paw, that's purty. (CARNES *starts to exit into house*) You shore fer sartin you can bear to let me go, Paw? (CARNES *turns.*)

PEDDLER   Are you *sure*, Mr. Carnes?

CARNES   Jist try to change my mind and see whut happens to you.
(*He takes a firmer grip on his gun and exits into the house.*)

ADO ANNIE   Oh, Ali Hakim, ain't it wonderful, Paw makin' up our mind fer us? He won't change neither. Onct he gives his word that you c'n have me, why you *got* me.

PEDDLER   I *know* I got you.

ADO ANNIE (*Starry-eyed*)   Mrs. Ali Hakim . . . the Peddler's bride. Wait till I tell the girls.
(*She exits. ALI leans against the porch post as the music starts. Then he starts to pace up and down, thinking hard, his head bowed, his hands behind his back. The orchestra starts a vamp that continues under the melody. Some men enter and watch him curiously, but he is unmindful of them until they start to sing. Throughout this entire number, the PEDDLER must be burning, and he transmits his indignation to the men who sing in a spirit of angry protest, by the time the refrain is reached.*)

PEDDLER (*Circling the stage*)
    Trapped! . . .
    Tricked! . . .
    Hoodblinked! . . .
    Hambushed! . . .

MEN
    Friend,
    Whut's on yer mind?
    Why do you walk

Around and around,
With yer hands
Folded behind,
And yer chin
Scrapin' the ground?
(*The* PEDDLER *walks away, then comes back to them and starts to pour out his heart.*)

PEDDLER

Twenty minutes ago I am free like a breeze,
Free like a bird in the woodland wild,
Free like a gypsy, free like a child,
I'm unattached!
Twenty minutes ago I can do what I please,
Flick my cigar ashes on a rug,
Dunk with a doughnut, drink from a jug—
I'm a happy man!
(*Crescendo*)
I'm minding my own business like I oughter,
Ain't meaning any harm to anyone.
I'm talking to a certain farmer's daughter—
Then I'm looking in the muzzle of a gun!

MEN

It's gittin' so you cain't have any fun!
Ev'ry daughter has a father with a gun!

It's a scandal, it's a outrage!
How a gal gits a husband today!

PEDDLER

If you make one mistake when the moon is bright,
Then they tie you to a contract, so you'll make it ev'ry night!

MEN

> It's a scandal, it's a outrage!
> When her fambly surround you and say:
> "You gotta take an' make a honest womern outa Nell!"

PEDDLER

> To make you make her honest, she will lie like hell!

MEN

> It's a scandal, it's a outrage!
> On our manhood, it's a blot!
> Where is the leader who will save us?
> And be the first man to be shot?

PEDDLER (*Spoken*)   Me?

MEN (*Spoken*)   Yes, you!
> (*Sing*)
> It's a scandal, it's a outrage!
> Jist a wink and a kiss and you're through!

PEDDLER

> You're a mess, and in less than a year, by heck!
> There's a baby on your shoulder making bubbles on your
>   neck!

MEN

> It's a scandal, it's a outrage!
> Any farmer will tell you it's true.

PEDDLER

> A rooster in a chickencoop is better off'n men.
> He ain't the special property of just one hen!

(ANNIE *and girls enter at side.*)

MEN

It's a scandal, it's a outrage!
It's a problem we must solve!
We gotta start a revolution!

GIRLS

All right, boys! Revolve!
(*The boys swing around, see the girls and are immediately
cowed. The girls pick them off the line and walk off with them,
to the music. All exit except one girl, who stalks around looking for a boy. Suddenly one appears, sees the girl and exits fast.
She pursues him like mad.* GERTIE *enters through gate with*
CURLY. LAUREY *enters on the porch and starts packing her
lunch hamper.*)

GERTIE   Hello, Laurey. Jist packin' yer hamper now?

LAUREY   I been busy.
(GERTIE *looks in* LAUREY's *hamper.* AUNT ELLER *enters.*)

GERTIE   You got gooseberry tarts, too. Wonder if they is as light
as mine. Mine'd like to float away if you blew on them.

LAUREY   I did blow on one of mine and it broke up into a million pieces.
(GERTIE *laughs—that laugh again.*)

GERTIE   Ain't she funny!
(*The girls step toward each other menacingly.*)

AUNT ELLER   Gertie! Better come inside, and cool off.

GERTIE   You comin' inside 'th me, Curly?

CURLY   Not jist yet.

GERTIE   Well, don't be too long. And don't fergit when the auction starts tonight, mine's the biggest hamper.
(*The laugh again, and she exits.*)

LAUREY (*Going on with her packing*)   So that's the Cummin's girl I heared so much talk of.

CURLY   You seen her before, ain't you?

LAUREY   Yeow. But not since she got so old. Never did see anybody get so peeked-lookin' in sich a short time.

AUNT ELLER (*Amused at* LAUREY)   Yeah, and she says she's only eighteen. I betcha she's nineteen.
(AUNT ELLER *exits.*)

CURLY   What yer got in yer hamper?

LAUREY   'At's jist some ole meat pies and apple jelly. Nothin' like whut Gertie Cummin's has in *her* basket.
(*She sits on the arm of a rocking chair.*)

CURLY   You really goin' to drive to the Box Social with that Jud feller?
(*Pause.*)

LAUREY   Reckon so. Why?

CURLY Nothin' . . . It's jist that ev'rybody seems to expec' *me* to take you.
(*He sits on the other arm of the rocker.*)

LAUREY Then, mebbe it's jist as well you ain't. We don't want people talkin' 'bout us, do we?

CURLY You think people *do* talk about us?

LAUREY Oh, you know how they air—like a swarm of mud-wasps. Alw'ys gotta be buzzin' 'bout sumpin.

CURLY (*Rocking the chair gaily*) Well, whut're they sayin'? That you're stuck on me?

LAUREY Uh-uh. Most of the talk is that you're stuck on me.

CURLY Cain't imagine how these ugly rumors start.

LAUREY Me neither.
(*Sings*)
Why do they think up stories that link my name with yours?

CURLY
Why do the neighbors gossip all day behind their doors?

LAUREY
I have a way to prove what they say is quite untrue;
Here is the gist, a practical list of "don'ts" for you:

Don't throw bouquets at me—
Don't please my folks too much,

Don't laugh at my jokes too much—
People will say we're in love!

CURLY (*Leaving her*)
   Who laughs at yer jokes?

LAUREY (*Following him*)
   Don't sigh and gaze at me,
   Your sighs are so like mine,
      (CURLY *turns to embrace her, she stops him*)
   Your eyes musn't glow like mine—
   People will say we're in love!
   Don't start collecting things—

CURLY
   Like whut?

LAUREY
   Give me my rose and my glove.
      (*He looks away, guiltily*)
   Sweetheart, they're suspecting things—
   People will say we're in love!

CURLY
   Some people claim that you are to blame as much as I—
      (*She is about to deny this*)
   Why do you take the trouble to bake my fav'rit pie?
      (*Now she looks guilty*)
   Grantin' your wish, I carved our initials on that tree . . .
      (*He points off at the tree*)
   Jist keep a slice of all that advice you give, so free!

Don't praise my charm too much,
Don't look so vain with me,
Don't stand in the rain with me,
People will say we're in love!
Don't take my arm too much,
Don't keep your hand in mine,
Your hand looks so grand in mine,
People will say we're in love!
Don't dance all night with me,
Till the stars fade from above.
They'll see it's all right with me,
People will say we're in love!
    (*Music continues as* CURLY *speaks*)
Don't you reckon y'could tell that Jud you'd ruther go with me tonight?

LAUREY Curly! I—no, I couldn't.

CURLY Oh, you couldn't? (*Frowning*) Think I'll go down here to the smokehouse, where Jud's at. See whut's so elegant about him, makes girls wanta go to parties 'th him.
    (*He starts off, angrily.*)

LAUREY Curly!

CURLY (*Turning*) Whut?

LAUREY Nothin'.
    (*She watches* CURLY *as he exits, then sits on rocker crying softly and starts to sing:*)
Don't sigh and gaze at me,
Your sighs are so like mine,

Your eyes mustn't glow like mine—
(*Music continues. She chokes up, can't go on.* AUNT ELLER *has come out and looks with great understanding.*)

AUNT ELLER   Got yer hamper packed?

LAUREY (*Snapping out of it*)   Oh, Aunt Eller. . . . Yes, nearly.

AUNT ELLER   Like a hanky?

LAUREY   Whut'd I want with a ole hanky?

AUNT ELLER (*Handing her hers*)   Y'got a smudge on yer cheek—
jist under yer eye.
(LAUREY *dries her eyes, starts toward the house, thinks about the bottle of "Lixir of Egyp'," picks it up, looks at* AUNT ELLER, *and runs out through the gate and off stage.* AUNT ELLER *sits in the rocker and hums the refrain, happy and contented, as lights dim and the curtain falls.*)

Scene II

SCENE: *The Smokehouse.*
Immediately after Scene I.
It is a dark, dirty building where the meat was once kept. The rafters are smoky, covered with dust and cobwebs. On a low loft many things are stored—horse collars, plow-shares, a binder twine, a keg of nails. Under it, the bed is grimy and never made. On the walls, tobacco advertisements, and pink covers off Police Gazettes. *In a corner there are hoes, rakes and an axe. Two chairs, a table and a spittoon comprise the furniture. There is a mirror for shaving, several farm lanterns and a rope. A small window lets in a little light, but not much.*
JUD *enters and crosses to table. There is a knock on the door. He rises quickly and tiptoes to the window to peek outside. Then he glides swiftly back to the table. Takes out a pistol and starts to polish it. There is a second knock.*

JUD (*Calling out sullenly*)   Well, open it, cain't you?

CURLY (*Opening the door and strolling in*)   Howdy.

JUD   Whut'd you want?

CURLY   I done got th'ough my business up here at the house. Jist thought I'd pay a call. (*Pause*) You got a gun, I see.

JUD   Good un. Colt forty-five.

CURLY   Whut do you do with it?

JUD   Shoot things.

CURLY   Oh. (*He moseys around the room casually*) That there pink picture—now that's a naked womern, ain't it?

JUD   Yer eyes don't lie to you.

CURLY   Plumb stark naked as a jaybird. No. No, she ain't. Not quite. Got a couple of thingumbobs tied onto her.

JUD   Shucks. That ain't a think to whut I got here. (*He shoves a pack of postcards across the table toward* CURLY) Lookit that top one.

CURLY (*Covering his eyes*)   I'll go blind! . . . (*Throwing it back on the table*) That ud give me idys, that would.

JUD (*Picking it up and looking at it*)   That's a dinger, that is.

CURLY (*Gravely*)   Yeah, that shore is a dinger. . . . (*Taking down a rope*) That's a good-lookin' rope you got there. (*He begins to spin it*) Spins nice. You know Will Parker? He can shore spin a rope. (*He tosses one end of the rope over the rafter and pulls down on both ends, tentatively*) 'S a good strong hook you got there. You could hang yerself on that, Jud.

JUD   I could whut?

CURLY (*Cheerfully*)   Hang yerself. It ud be as easy as fallin' off a log! Fact is, you could stand on a log—er a cheer if you'd rather—right about here—see? And put this here around yer neck. Tie that good up there first, of course. Then all you'd have to do would be to fall off the log—er the cheer, whichever you'd ruther fall off of. In five minutes, or less, with good luck, you'd be daid as a doornail.

JUD   Whut'd you mean by that?

CURLY   Nen folks ud come to yer funril and sing sad songs.

JUD (*Disdainfully*)   Yamnh!

CURLY   They would. You never know how many people like you till you're daid. Y'd prob'ly be laid out in the parlor. Y'd be all diked out in yer best suit with yer hair combed down slick, and a high starched collar.

JUD (*Beginning to get interested*)   Would they be any flowers, d'you think?

CURLY   Shore would, and palms, too—all around yer cawfin. Nen folks ud stand around you and the men ud bare their heads and the womern ud sniffle softly. Some'd prob'ly faint—ones that had tuck a shine to you when you wuz alive.

JUD   Whut womern have tuck a shine to me?

CURLY   Lots of womern. On'y they don't never come right out and show you how they feel less'n you die first.

JUD (*Thoughtfully*)   I guess that's so.

CURLY   They'd shore sing loud though when the singin' started—
sing like their hearts ud break!
>   (*He starts to sing very earnestly and solemnly, improvising the
>   sort of thing he thinks might be sung:*)
>   Pore Jud is daid,
>   Pore Jud Fry is daid!
>   All gether 'round his cawfin now and cry.
>   He had a heart of gold
>   And he wasn't very old—
>   Oh, why did sich a feller have to die?
>   Pore Jud is daid,
>   Pore Jud Fry is daid!
>   He's lookin', oh, so peaceful and serene.

JUD   (*Touched and suddenly carried away, he sings a soft response*)
>   And serene!
>   (*Takes off hat.*)

CURLY

>   He's all laid out to rest
>   With his hands acrost his chest.
>   His fingernails have never b'en so clean!
>   (JUD *turns slowly to question the good taste of this last reference,
>   but* CURLY *plunges straight into another item of the imagined
>   wake*)

Nen the preacher'd git up and he'd say: "Folks! We are gethered
here to moan and groan over our brother Jud Fry who hung
hisse'f by a rope in the smokehouse." Nen there'd be weepin'
and wailin' (*Significantly*) from some of those womern.
>   (JUD *nods his head understandingly*)

Nen he'd say, "Jud was the most misunderstood man in the
territory. People useter think he was a mean, ugly feller.

(JUD *looks up*)
And they called him a dirty skunk and a ornery pig-stealer.
(CURLY *switches quickly*)
But—the folks 'at really knowed him, knowed 'at beneath
them two dirty shirts he alw'ys wore, there beat a heart as big
as all outdoors.

JUD (*Repeating reverently as if at a revivalist meeting*)   As big as
all outdoors.

CURLY   Jud Fry loved his fellow man.

JUD   He loved his fellow man.

CURLY (CURLY *is warming up and speaks with the impassioned in-
flections of an evangelist*)   He loved the birds of the forest
and the beasts of the field. He loved the mice and the vermin
in the barn, and he treated the rats like equals—which was
right. And—he loved little children. He loved ev'body and
ev'thin' in the world! . . . On'y he never let on, so nobody ever
knowed it!
    (*Returning to vigorous song:*)
    Pore Jud is daid,
    Pore Jud Fry is daid!
    His friends'll weep and wail fer miles around.

JUD (*Now right into it*)
    Miles around.

CURLY
    The daisies in the dell
    Will give out a diff'runt smell

Becuz pore Jud is underneath the ground.
(JUD *is too emotionally exalted by the spirit of* CURLY*'s singing to be analytical. He now takes up a refrain of his own.*)

JUD
Pore Jud is daid,
A candle lights his haid,
He's layin' in a cawfin made of wood.

CURLY
Wood.

JUD
And folks are feelin' sad
Cuz they useter treat him bad,
And now they know their friend has gone fer good.

CURLY (*Softly*)
Good.

JUD AND CURLY
Pore Jud is dead,
A candle lights his haid!

CURLY
He's lookin', oh, so purty and so nice.
He looks like he's asleep.
It's a shame that he won't keep,
But it's summer and we're runnin' out of ice . . .
Pore Jud—Pore Jud!
(JUD *breaks down, weeps, and sits at the table, burying his head in his arms*)

Yes, sir. That's the way it ud be. Shore be a interestin' funril. Wouldn't like to miss it.

JUD (*His eyes narrowing*)   Wouldn't like to miss it, eh? Well, mebbe you will. (*He resumes polishing the gun*) Mebbe you'll go first.

CURLY (*Sitting down*)   Mebbe. . . . Le's see now, whur did you work at before you come here? Up by Quapaw, wasn't it?

JUD   Yes, and before that over by Tulsa. Lousy they was to me. Both of 'em. Always makin' out they was better. Treatin' me like dirt.

CURLY   And whut'd you do—git even?

JUD   Who said anythin' about gittin' even?

CURLY   No one, that I recollect. It jist come into my head.

JUD   If it ever come to gittin' even with anybody, I'd know how to do it.

CURLY   That?
     (*Looking down at gun and pointing.*)

JUD   Nanh! They's safer ways then that, if you use yer brains . . . 'Member that f'ar on the Bartlett farm over by Sweetwater?

CURLY   Shore do. 'Bout five years ago. Turrible accident. Burned up the father and mother and daughter.

JUD   That warn't no accident. A feller told me—the h'ard hand was stuck on the Bartlett girl, and he found her in the hayloft with another feller.

CURLY   And it was him that burned the place?

JUD (*Nodding*)   It tuck him weeks to git all the kerosene—buying it at different times—feller who told me made out it happened in Missouri, but I knowed all the time it was the Bartlett farm. Whut a liar he was!

CURLY   And a kind of a—a kind of a murderer, too. Wasn't he? (CURLY *rises, goes over to the door and opens it*) Git a little air in here.

JUD   You ain't told me yet whut business you had here. We got no cattle to sell ner no cow ponies. The oat crop is done spoke fer.

CURLY   You shore relieved my mind consid'able.

JUD (*Tensely*)   They's on'y one other thing on this farm you could want—and it better not be that!

CURLY (*Closing the door deliberately and turning slowly, to face* JUD)   But that's jist whut it is.

JUD   Better not be! You keep away from her, you hear?

CURLY (*Coolly*)   You know somebody orta tell Laurey whut kind of a man you air. And fer that matter, somebody orta tell *you* onct about yerself.

JUD You better git outa here, Curly.

CURLY A feller wouldn't feel very safe in here with you . . . 'f
he didn't know you. (*Acidly*) But I know you, Jud. (CURLY
looks him straight in the eye) In this country, they's two things
you c'n do if you're a man. Live out of doors is one. Live in
a hole is the other. I've set by my horse in the bresh som'eres
and heared a rattlesnake many a time. Rattle, rattle, rattle!—
he'd go, skeered to death. Somebody comin' close to his hole!
Somebody gonna step on him! Git his old fangs ready, full of
pizen! Curl up and wait!—Long's you live in a hole, you're
skeered, you got to have pertection. You c'n have muscles, oh,
like arn—and still be as weak as a empty bladder—less'n you
got things to barb yer hide with. (*Suddenly, harshly, directly to*
JUD) How'd you git to be the way you air, anyway—settin' here
in this filthy hole—and thinkin' the way you're thinkin'? Why
don't you do sumpin healthy onct in a while, 'stid of stayin'
shet up here—a-crawlin' and festerin'!

JUD Anh!
(*He seizes a gun in a kind of reflex, a kind of desperate frenzy,
and pulls the trigger. Luckily the gun is pointed toward the
ceiling.*)

CURLY (*Actually in a state of high excitement, but outwardly cool and
calm, he draws his own gun*) You orta feel better now. Hard
on the roof, though. I wisht you'd let me show you sumpin.
(JUD *doesn't move, but stands staring into* CURLY'*s eyes*) They's a
knot-hole over there about as big as a dime. See it a-winkin'?
I jist want to see if I c'n hit it. (*Unhurriedly, with cat-like ten-
sion, he turns and fires at the wall high up*) Bullet right through
the knot-hole, 'thout tetchin', slick as a whistle, didn't I? I

knowed I could do it. You saw it, too, didn't you? (*Ad lib off stage*) Somebody's a-comin', I 'spect.
(*He listens.* JUD *looks at the floor.* AUNT ELLER, *the* PEDDLER *and several others come running in.*)

AUNT ELLER (*Gasping for breath*)   Who f'ard off a gun? Was that you, Curly? Don't set there, you lummy, answer when you're spoke to.

CURLY   Well, I shot onct.

AUNT ELLER   What was you shootin' at?

CURLY (*Rises*)   See that knot-hole over there?

AUNT ELLER   I see lots of knot-holes.

CURLY   Well, it was one of them.

AUNT ELLER (*Exasperated*)   Well, ain't you a pair of purty nuthin's, a-pickin' away at knot-holes and skeerin' everybody to death! Orta give you a good Dutch rub and arn some of the craziness out of you! (*Calling off to people in doorway*) 'S all right! Nobody hurt. Jist a pair of fools swappin' noises.
(*She exits.*)

PEDDLER   Mind if I visit with you, gents? It's good to get away from the women for a while. Now then, we're all by ourselves. I got a few purties, private knickknacks for to show you. Special for the menfolks.
(*Starts to get them out.*)

CURLY See you gentlemen later. I gotta git a surrey I h'ard fer tonight.
(*He starts to go.*)

PEDDLER (*Shoving cards under* JUD's *nose*) Art postcards.

JUD Who you think yer takin' in that surrey?

CURLY Aunt Eller—and Laurey, if she'll come with me.

JUD She won't.

CURLY Mebbe she will.
(*Exits.*)

JUD (*Raising his voice after* CURLY) She promised to go with me, and she better not change her mind. She better not!

PEDDLER Now, I want ye to look at these straight from Paris.

JUD I don't want none o' them things now. Got any frog-stickers?

PEDDLER You mean one of them long knives? What would you want with a thing like that?

JUD I dunno. Kill a hog—er a skunk. It's all the same, ain't it? I tell you whut I'd like better'n a frog-sticker, if you got one. Ever hear of one of them things you call "The Little Wonder"? It's a thing you hold up to your eyes to see pitchers, only that ain't all they is to it . . . not quite. Y'see it's got a little jigger onto it, and you tetch it and out springs a sharp blade.

PEDDLER   On a spring, eh?

JUD   Y'say to a feller, "Look through this." Nen when he's lookin' you snap out the blade. It's jist above his chest and, bang! Down you come.
(*Slaps the* PEDDLER *on the chest, knocking the wind from him.*)

PEDDLER (*After recovering from the blow*)   A good joke to play on a friend . . . I—er—don't handle things like that. Too dangerous. What I'd like to show you is my new stock of postcards.

JUD   Don't want none. Sick of them things. I'm going to get me a real womern.

PEDDLER   What would you want with a woman? Why, I'm having trouble right now, all on account of a woman. They always make trouble. And you say you *want* one. Why? Look at you! You're a man what is free to come and go as you please. You got a nice cozy little place. (*Looking place over*) Private. Nobody to bother you. Artistic pictures. They don't talk back to you. . . .

JUD   I'm t'ard of all these *pitchers* of women!

PEDDLER   All right. You're tired of them. So throw 'em away and buy some new ones. (*Showing him cards again*) You get tired of a woman and what can you do? Nothing! Just keep getting tireder and tireder!

Alfred Drake and Joan Roberts from the original Broadway production (1943).

Members of the original Broadway cast, including (gathered around the surrey, from left to right) Lee Dixon, Celeste Holm, Alfred Drake, Joan Roberts, Joseph Buloff (kneeling), and Betty Garde.

The "postcard girls" from Laurey's "Dream Ballet," original Broadway cast.

Original Broadway cast.

December 4, 1947: Richard Rodgers conducts the 2,000th performance of *Oklahoma!* on Broadway.

The Rivoli Theater in New York hosts the premiere engagement of the film (1955).

Gordon MacRae and Shirley Jones in the 1955 film version.

Shirley Jones in the film.

Agnes de Mille's "Dream Ballet" from Broadway, adapted for the film version.

Hugh Jackman and Josefina Gabrielle from the 1998 Royal National Theatre of Great Britain production.

The company from the Royal National Theatre production.

Josefina Gabrielle and Vicki Simon, Royal National Theatre.

Maureen Lipman and Hugh Jackman, Royal National Theatre.

Patrick Wilson and Josefina Gabrielle, from the 2002 Broadway production.

Justin Bohon, Broadway, 2002.

Patrick Wilson, center, and the ensemble, Broadway, 2002.

JUD   I made up my mind.

PEDDLER (*Packing his bag and starting off*)   So you want a real
woman. . . . Say, do you happen to know a girl named Ado
Annie?

JUD   I don't want her.

PEDDLER   I don't want her either. But I got her!
(*Exit.*)

JUD   Don't want nuthin' from no peddler. Want real things! Whut
am I doin' shet up here—like that feller says—a-crawlin' and
a-festerin'? Whut am I doin' in this lousy smokehouse?
(*He looks about the room, scowling. Then he starts to sing, half
talking at first, then singing in full voice:*)
The floor creaks,
The door squeaks,
There's a fieldmouse a-nibblin' on a broom,
And I set by myself
Like a cobweb on a shelf,
By myself in a lonely room.

But when there's a moon in my winder
And it slants down a beam 'crost my bed,
Then the shadder of a tree starts a-dancin' on the wall
And a dream starts a-dancin' in my head.
And all the things that I wish fer
Turn out like I want them to be,
And I'm better'n that Smart Aleck cowhand
Who thinks he is better'n me!
And the girl that I want

Ain't afraid of my arms,
And her own soft arms keep me warm.
And her long, yeller hair
Falls acrost my face
Jist like the rain in a storm!

The floor creaks,
The door squeaks,
And the mouse starts a-nibblin' on the broom.
And the sun flicks my eyes—
It was all a pack o' lies!
I'm awake in a lonely room. . . .

I ain't gonna dream 'bout her arms no more!
I ain't gonna leave her alone!
Goin' outside,
Git myself a bride,
Git me a womern to call my own.

End of Scene II

Scene III

AT RISE: *A grove on* LAUREY'*s farm. Singing girls and* GERTIE *seated under tree. A girl,* VIVIAN, *is telling* GERTIE'*s fortune.*

VIVIAN   And to yer house a dark clubman!
  (*Laughter from girls.* LAUREY *enters.*)

LAUREY   Girls, could you—could you go som'eres else and tell fortunes? I gotta be here by myself.

GERTIE (*Pointing to bottle*)   Look! She bought 'at ole smellin' salts the peddler tried to sell us!

LAUREY   It ain't smellin' salts. It's goin' to make up my mind fer me. Lookit me take a good whiff now!
  (*She chokes on it.*)

GERTIE   That's the camphor.

LAUREY   Please, girls, go away.
  (GERTIE *laughs and exits.* LAUREY *closes her eyes tight.*)

ELLEN   Hey, Laurey, is it true you're lettin' Jud take you tonight 'stid of Curly?

LAUREY   Tell you better when I think ever'thin' out clear. Beginnin' to see things clear a'ready.

KATE I c'n tell you whut you want . . .
(*Singing*)
Out of your dreams and into his arms you long to fly.

ELLEN
You don't need Egyptian smellin' salts to tell you why!

KATE
Out of your dreams and into the hush of falling shadows.

VIRGINIA
When the mist is low, and stars are breaking through,

VIVIAN
Then out of your dreams you'll go.

ALL THE GIRLS
Into a dream come true.
Make up your mind, make up your mind, Laurey, Laurey
dear.
Make up your own, make up your own story, Laurey dear.
Ol' Pharaoh's daughter won't tell you what to do.
Ask your heart—whatever it tells you will be true.
(*They drift off as* LAUREY *sings.*)

LAUREY
Out of my dreams and into your arms I long to fly.
I will come as evening comes to woo a waiting sky.
Out of my dreams and into the hush of falling shadows,
When the mist is low, and stars are breaking through,
Then out of my dreams I'll go,
Into a dream with you.

BALLET (*The things* LAUREY *sees in her dream that help her "make up her mind."*)
(*During the above refrain the lights dim to a spot on* LAUREY. CURLY *enters in another spot, walking slowly and standing perfectly still. Then his ballet counterpart enters and stands behind him.* LAUREY'*s ballet counterpart enters and stands behind her. These are figures fading into her dream. The real* CURLY *and the real* LAUREY *back off slowly, and leave the stage to their counterparts who move toward the center and into an embrace. The downstage drop is lifted and they are in another scene, full stage.*

These dream figures of LAUREY *and* CURLY *dance ecstatically. A young girl enters, sees them and bounds off to break the news and soon others dance on and off gaily. Two of* CURLY'*s cowboy friends stroll by and wave their greeting. "Curly" kisses "Laurey" again and walks away, happy and smug.*

A little girl runs on, presents "Laurey" with a nosegay and then bursts into tears. More girl friends dance on and embrace her. A bridal veil floats down from the skies and they place it on her head. "Curly" and the boys enter, in the manner of cowboys astride their horses. Following a gay dance, the music slows to wedding-march tempo. "Curly," a serious expression on his face, awaits his bride who walks down an aisle formed by the girls.

Now the ballet counterpart of JUD *walks slowly forward and takes off "Laurey's" veil. Expecting to see her lover,* CURLY, *she looks up and finds "Jud." Horrified, she backs away. Her friends, with stony faces, look straight ahead of them. "Curly," too, is stern and austere and when she appeals to him, he backs away from her. All of them leave her. She is alone with "Jud."*

"Jud" starts to dance with her but he is soon diverted by the entrance of three dance-hall girls who look very much like the Police Gazette *pictures* LAUREY *has seen tacked on to his walls in the smokehouse. Some of the cowboys follow the girls on, and whistle at them. But that is as far as they go. The cowboys are timid and inexpert in handling these sophisticated women. The women do an amusing, satirically bawdy dance. Then "Jud" and the boys dance with them.*

After the girls dance off, "Laurey" and "Jud" are again alone. "Curly" enters, and the long-awaited conflict with "Jud" is now unavoidable. "Curly," his hand holding an imaginary pistol, fires at "Jud" again and again, but "Jud" keeps slowly advancing on him, immune to bullets. He lifts "Curly" in the air and throws him to the ground. A fierce fight ensues. The friends of LAUREY *and* CURLY *run helplessly from one side to the other. Just when the tables seem to have turned in "Curly's" favor, "Jud" gets a death grip on his throat. He is killing "Curly." "Laurey" runs up to him and begs him to release her lover. It is clear by her pantomime that she will give herself to* JUD *to save* CURLY. *"Jud" drops "Curly's" limp body, picks up "Laurey" and carries her away. Over "Jud's" shoulder she blows a feeble, heartbroken kiss to "Curly's" prostrate form on the ground. The crowd surround him and carry him off in the dark as a spot comes up revealing the* real LAUREY *being shaken out of her dream by the* real JUD.)

JUD   Wake up, Laurey. It's time to start fer the party.
(*As she awakens and starts mechanically to go with* JUD, *the*

real CURLY *enters expectantly. She hesitates.* JUD *holds out his arm and scowls. Remembering the disaster of her recent dream, she avoids its reality by taking* JUD*'s arm and going with him, looking wistfully back at* CURLY *with the same sad eyes that her ballet counterpart had on her exit.* CURLY *stands alone, puzzled, dejected and defeated, as the curtain falls.)*

ACT TWO

Scene I

SCENE: *The* SKIDMORE *ranch.*

SKIDMORE'*s guests dancing a* "*set.*" *Soon after the curtain rises, the melody settles into a* "*vamp*" *and* CARNES *holds up his hand as a signal that he wants to sing. The dancing couples retire and listen to him.*

CARNES
The farmer and the cowman should be friends,
Oh, the farmer and the cowman should be friends.
One man likes to push a plow,
The other likes to chase a cow,
But that's no reason why they cain't be friends.

Territory folks should stick together,
Territory folks should all be pals.
Cowboys, dance with the farmers' daughters!
Farmers, dance with the ranchers' gals!
    (*The chorus repeats this last quatrain*)
    (*They dance with gusto—sixteen measures—then the vamp is resumed and* CARNES *starts to sing again*)
I'd like to say a word fer the farmer.

AUNT ELLER (*Spoken*)   Well, say it.

CARNES   He come out west and made a lot of changes.

WILL (*Scornfully; singing*)
He come out west and built a lot of fences!

CURLY
And built 'em right acrost our cattle ranges!

CORD ELAM (*A cowman; spoken*)   Whyn't those dirtscratchers stay in Missouri where they belong?

FARMER (*Spoken*)   We got as much right here—

CARNES (*Shouting*)   Gentlemen—shut up!
(*Quiet restored, he resumes singing*)
The farmer is a good and thrifty citizen.

FRED (*Spoken*)   He's thrifty, all right.

CARNES (*Glaring at* FRED, *he continues with song*)
No matter whut the cowman says or thinks,
You seldom see him drinkin' in a barroom—

CURLY
Unless somebody else is buyin' drinks!

CARNES (*Barging in quickly to save the party's respectability*)
The farmer and the cowman should be friends,
Oh, the farmer and the cowman should be friends.
The cowman ropes a cow with ease,
The farmer steals her butter and cheese,
But that's no reason why they cain't be friends!

ALL
Territory folks should stick together,
Territory folks should all be pals.
Cowboys, dance with the farmers' daughters!

Farmers, dance with the ranchers' gals!
(*Dance, as before. Then back to the vamp.*)

AUNT ELLER (*Singing*)
I'd like to say a word fer the cowboy . . .

FARMER (*Anxious to get back at the cowmen; spoken*)   Oh, you
would!

AUNT ELLER
The road he treads is difficult and stony.
He rides fer days on end
With jist a pony fer a friend. . . .

ADO ANNIE
I shore am feelin' sorry fer the pony.

AUNT ELLER
The farmer should be sociable with the cowboy,
If he rides by and asks fer food and water.
Don't treat him like a louse,
Make him welcome in yer house . . .

CARNES
But be shore that you lock up yer wife and daughter!
(*Laughs, jibes, protests.*)

CORD ELAM (*Spoken from here on*)   Who wants a ole farm womern anyway?

ADO ANNIE   Notice you married one, so's you c'd git a square
meal!

MAN (*To* CORD ELAM)   You cain't talk that-a-way 'bout our womern folks!

WILL   He can say whut he wants.
>   (WILL *hauls off on him and a free-for-all fight ensues, all the*
>   *men mixing with one another, the women striving vainly to*
>   *keep peace by singing "The farmer and the cowman should be*
>   *friends!")*
>   (AUNT ELLER *grabs a gun from some man's holster and fires it.*
>   *This freezes the picture. A still, startled crowd stops and looks*
>   *to see who's been shot.* AUNT ELLER *strides forward, separating*
>   *the fighters, pulling them away from one another, and none*
>   *too gently.)*

AUNT ELLER   They ain't nobody goin' to slug out anythin'—this
here's a party! (*Pointing the gun at* CARNES) Sing it, Andrew!
Dum tiddy um tum tum—

CARNES (*Frightened, obeys*)
The farmer and the cowman should be friends . . .
>   (AUNT ELLER *points her gun at a group, and conducts them.*
>   *They join in quickly.*)

RIGHT GROUP
Oh, the farmer and the cowman should be friends.
>   (*She turns her gun on left group and now they all sing.*)

ALL
One man likes to push a plow,
The other likes to chase a cow,
But that's no reason why they cain't be friends!
>   (IKE *comes down and joins* AUNT ELLER *and* CARNES.)

IKE

And when this territory is a state,
And jines the union jist like all the others,
The farmer and the cowman and the merchant
Must all behave theirsel's and act like brothers.

AUNT ELLER

I'd like to teach you all a little sayin'—
And learn these words by heart the way you should:
"I don't say I'm no better than anybody else,
But I'll be damned if I ain't jist as good!"
(*They cheer the sentiment, and repeat lustily:*)

ALL

I don't say I'm no better than anybody else,
But I'll be damned if I ain't jist as good!
Territory folks should stick together,
Territory folks should all be pals.
Cowboys, dance with the farmers' daughters!
Farmers, dance with the ranchers' gals!
(*Now they go into a gay, unrestrained dance.*)

IKE (*After number is over*)   C'mon, everybody! Time to start the Box Social.

CORD ELAM   I'm so hungry I c'd eat a gatepost.

DOROTHY   Who's goin' to be the auctioneer?

TOM   Aunt Eller!
(*Shouts of approval from the entire crowd.*)

AUNT ELLER (*Playing coy*)   Let one of the men be the auctioneer.

CROWD   "No, Aunt Eller, yore the best." "Ain't any ole men auctioneers as good as you."

AUNT ELLER   All right then. Now you know the rules, gentlemen. Y'got to bid blind. Y'ain't s'posed to know whut girl goes with whut hamper. Of course, if yer sweetheart has told you that hers'll be done up in a certain kind of way with a certain color ribbon, that ain't my fault. Now we'll auction all the hampers on t'other side of the house and work around back here. Follow me.

> (AUNT ELLER *starts off, followed by the crowd. As the crowd exits, the* PEDDLER *strolls on, meeting* WILL *ambling along with his bag.*)

PEDDLER   Hello, young fellow.

WILL   Oh, it's you!

PEDDLER   I was just hoping to meet up with you. It seems like you and me ought to have a little talk.

WILL   We only got one thing to talk about. Well, Mr. Hakim, I hear you got yerself engaged to Ado Annie.

PEDDLER   Well . . .

WILL   Well, nothin'. I don't know what to call you. You ain't purty enough fer a skunk. You ain't skinny enough fer a snake. You're too little to be a man, and too big to be a mouse. I reckon you're a rat.

PEDDLER   That's logical.

WILL   Answer me one question. Do you really love her?

PEDDLER   Well . . .

WILL   'Cuz if I thought you didn't I'd tie you up in this bag and
drop you in the river. Are you serious about her?

PEDDLER   Yes, I'm serious.

WILL   And do you worship the ground she walks on, like I do?
You better say yes!

PEDDLER   Yes—yes—yes.

WILL   The hell you do!

PEDDLER   Yes.

WILL   Would you spend every cent you had fer her? That's whut
I did. See that bag? Full of presents. Cost fifty bucks. All I had
in the world.

PEDDLER   If you had that fifty dollars cash . . .

WILL   I'd have Ado Annie, and you'd lose her.

PEDDLER (*Thoughtfully*)   Yes. I'd lose her. Let's see what you got
in here. Might want to buy something.

WILL   What would you want with them?

PEDDLER   I'm a peddler, ain't I? I buy and sell. Maybe pay you real money. . . . (*Significantly*) Maybe as much as—well, a lot. (WILL *becomes thoughtful. The* PEDDLER *fishes in bag and pulls out an item*) Ah, what a beautiful hot-water bag. It looks French. Must have cost plenty. I'll give you eight dollars for it.

WILL   Eight dollars? That wouldn't be honest. I only paid three-fifty.

PEDDLER   All right. I said I'd give you eight and I will. . . . (*The* PEDDLER *pulls a nightgown out of the bag. It is made of white lawn and is notable for a profusion of ribbons and bows on the neckline*) Say! That's a cracker-jake!

WILL   Take your hands off that! (*Grabbing it and holding it in front of him*) That wuz fer our weddin' night!

PEDDLER   It don't fit you so good. I'll pay you twenty-two dollars.

WILL   But that's—

PEDDLER   All right then—twenty-two-fifty! (*Stuffing it into his coat with the hot-water bag*) Not a cent more.
   (WILL *smiles craftily and starts to count on his fingers. The* PEDDLER *now pulls out a pair of corsets.*)

WILL   Them—those—that was fer her to wear.

PEDDLER   I didn't hardly think they was for you. (*Looking at them*) Mighty dainty. (*Putting them aside*) Fifteen dollars. Le's

see, eight and twenty-two makes thirty and fifteen is forty-five
and fifty cents is forty-five-fifty.
(*He looks craftily at* WILL *out of the corner of his eye and watches
the idea percolate through* WILL's *thick head.*)

WILL   Forty-five-fifty? Say, that's almos'—that's . . . (*Turning
anxiously*) Want to buy some more?

PEDDLER   Might.

WILL (*Taking "The Little Wonder" out of his pocket*)   D'you ever
see one of these?

PEDDLER (*Frightened*)   What made you buy this? Got it *in* for
somebody?

WILL   How d'you mean? It's jist funny pitchers.

PEDDLER (*Examining it carefully*)   That all you think it is? Well,
it's more'n that! It's . . .
(*He breaks off as* LAUREY *runs on, a frightened look on her
face.*)

LAUREY   Whur is ev'ybody? Whur's Aunt Eller?

WILL   On t'other side of the house, Laurey.

JUD (*Off stage*)   Laurey! Whur'd you run to?
(LAUREY *runs off, around the end of the house, putting hamper
on porch.*)

WILL   How much'll you give me fer that thing?

PEDDLER   I don't like to handle things like this. I guess you don't know what it really is.

WILL   Shore do. It's jist a girl in pink tights.

JUD (*Entering, carrying* LAUREY'*s basket*)   Either of you two see Laurey?

WILL   Jist went to th' other side of the house. Auction's goin' on there.
(JUD *grunts and starts upstage.*)

PEDDLER (*Calling to him*)   Hey, Jud! Here's one of them things you was looking for. "The Little Wonder."
(JUD *comes back and examines it.*)

JUD (*To* WILL)   How much?

WILL (*Closing his eyes to struggle with a mathematical problem*)   Three dollars and fifty cents.

JUD (*Digging in his pocket*)   Lotta money but I got an idy it might be worth it.
(JUD *goes upstage to look it over, then exits.*)

WILL   Let's see, three-fifty from him and forty-five-fifty from you. 'At makes fifty dollars, don't it?

PEDDLER   No. One dollar short.

WILL   Darn it. I musta figgered wrong. (*Impulsively*) How much fer all the resta the stuff in this bag?

PEDDLER (*Having the cash all ready*)   One dollar!

WILL   Done! Now I got fifty dollars, ain't I? Know whut that means? Means I'm goin' to take Ado Annie back from you!

PEDDLER   You wouldn't do a thing like that to me!

WILL   Oh, wouldn't I? And when I tell her paw who I got mosta the money offa, mebbe he'll change his mind 'bout who's smart and who's dumb!

PEDDLER   Say, young feller, you certainly bunkoed me!
(*Off right, there is a hum of voices and the crowd starts to drift on.* AUNT ELLER *enters, followed by the balance of the party.* JUD *eyes* LAUREY *throughout the ensuing dialogue.* CURLY *stands apart and pays little attention to anybody or anything.*)

AUNT ELLER   Now, here's the last two hampers. Whose they are I ain't got no idy!

ADO ANNIE (*In a loud voice*)   The little un's mine! And the one next to it is Laurey's!
(*General laughter.*)

AUNT ELLER   Well, that's the end of *that* secret. Now whut am I bid then fer Ado Annie's hamper?

SLIM   Two bits.

CORD ELAM   Four.

AUNT ELLER   Who says six? You, Slim? (SLIM *shakes his head*)

Ain't nobody hungry no more?—Whut about you, Peddler-
man? Six bits?

(*Pause.*)

PEDDLER Naw!

(CARNES *takes a gun from his pocket and prods the* PEDDLER
in the back.)

CARNES Come on.

PEDDLER Six bits!

AUNT ELLER Six bits ain't enough fer a lunch like Ado Annie
c'n make. Le's hear a dollar. How about you, Mike? You won
her last year.

MIKE Yeah. That's right. Hey, Ado Annie, y'got that same sweet-
pertater pie like last year?

ADO ANNIE You bet.

AUNT ELLER Same old sweet-pertater pie, Mike. Whut d'you
say?

MIKE I say it give me a three-day bellyache!

AUNT ELLER Never mind about that. Who bids a dollar?

CARNES (*Whispering to* PEDDLER) Bid!

PEDDLER (*Whispering back*) Mine's the last bid. I got her fer
six bits.

CARNES Bid a dollar.

(*The* PEDDLER *looks doubtful.* CARNES *prods him with his gun.*)

PEDDLER Ninety cents.

AUNT ELLER Ninety cents, we're gittin' rich. 'Nother desk fer th' schoolhouse. Do I hear more?

WILL (*Dramatically, his chin thrust forward*) You hear fifty dollars!

PEDDLER (*Immediately alarmed*) Hey!

AUNT ELLER Fifty dollars! Nobody ever bid fifty dollars for a lunch! Nobody ever bid ten.

CARNES He ain't got fifty dollars.

WILL Oh, yes, I have. (*Producing the money*) And 'f yer a man of honor y'gotta say Ado Annie b'longs to me, like y'said she would!

CARNES But where's yer money?

WILL (*Shoving out his hand*) Right here in my hand.

CARNES 'At ain't yours! Y'jist bid it, didn't you? Jist give it to th' schoolhouse. (*To* PEDDLER, *chuckling. Back to* WILL) Got to say the Peddler still gits my daughter's hand.

WILL Now wait a minute. That ain't fair!

AUNT ELLER   Goin' fer fifty dollars! Goin' . . .

PEDDLER (*Gulping*)   Fifty-one dollars!
(*A sensation, all turn to* PEDDLER.)

CARNES   You crazy?

WILL (*Mechanically*)   Fif— (*Prompted by frantic signs from the* PEDDLER, *he stops and suddenly realizes the significance of the* PEDDLER*'s bid*) Wait a minute. Wait! 'F I don't bid any more I c'n keep my money, cain't I?

AUNT ELLER (*Grinning*)   Shore can.

WILL   Nen I still got fifty dollars. (*Waving it in front of* CARNES) This is mine!

CARNES (*To* PEDDLER)   You feeble-minded shike-poke!

AUNT ELLER   Goin', goin', gone fer fifty-one dollars and 'at means Ado Annie'll git the prize, I guess.

WILL   And I git Ado Annie!

CARNES (*To* PEDDLER)   And whut're you gittin' fer yer fifty-one dollars?

PEDDLER (*Shrugging his shoulders*)   A three-day bellyache!
(PEDDLER *and* ADO ANNIE *pick up her basket and leave* AUNT ELLER.)

AUNT ELLER   Now here's my niece's hamper. (*General murmur of excitement runs through the crowd*) I took a peek inside a while ago and I must say it looks mighty tasty. Whut do I hear, gents?

SLIM   Two bits!

FRED   Four bits!

AUNT ELLER   Whut d'you say, Slim? Six?
(SLIM *shakes his head.*)

CARNES   I bid one dollar.

AUNT ELLER   More like it! Do I hear two?

JUD   A dollar and a quarter.
(LAUREY *gets a start from his voice.*)

CORD ELAM   Two dollars.

JOE   Two-fifty.

CARNES   Three dollars!

JUD   And two bits.

CORD ELAM   Three dollars and four bits!

JOE   Four dollars.

JUD (*Doggedly*)   And two bits.
(LAUREY *looks straight ahead of her, grimly.* AUNT ELLER *catches this look and a deep worry comes into her eyes.*)

AUNT ELLER   Four dollars and a quarter. (*Looking at* CURLY, *an appeal in her voice*) Ain't I goin' to hear any more?
(CURLY *turns and walks off, cool and deliberate*)
(LAUREY *bites her lip.* AUNT ELLER'*s voice has panic in it*)
I got a bid of four and a quarter—from Jud Fry. You goin' to let him have it?

CARNES   Four and a half.

AUNT ELLER (*Shouting, as if she were cheering*)   Four and a half! Goin' fer four and a half! Goin' . . .

JUD   Four-seventy-five.

AUNT ELLER (*Deflated*)   Four-seventy-five, come on, gentlemen. Schoolhouse ain't built yet. Got to git a nice chimbley.

CORD ELAM   Five dollars.

AUNT ELLER   Goin' fer five dollars! Goin' . . .

JUD   And two bits.

CORD ELAM   Too rich for my blood! Cain't afford no more.

AUNT ELLER (*Worried*)   Five and a quarter! Ain't got nearly enough yet. (*Looking at* CARNES) Not fer cold duck with stuffin' and that lemon-meringue pie.

CARNES   Six dollars.

AUNT ELLER   Six dollars! Goin' . . .

JUD   And two bits.

AUNT ELLER   My, you're stubborn, Jud. Mr. Carnes is a richer man'n you. (*Looking at* CARNES) And I know he likes custard with raspberry syrup. (*Pause. No one bids*) Anybody goin' to bid any more?

JUD   No. They all dropped out. Cain't you see?

FRED   You got enough, Aunt Eller.

CARNES   Let's git on.

JUD   Here's the money.

AUNT ELLER (*Looking off*)   Hold on, you! I ain't said "Goin', goin', gone" yet!

JUD   Well, say it!

AUNT ELLER (*Speaking slowly*)   Goin' to Jud fer six dollars and two bits! Goin' . . .
    (CURLY *enters, a saddle over his arm.*)

CURLY   Who'd you say was gittin' Laurey?

AUNT ELLER   Jud Fry.

CURLY   And fer how much?

AUNT ELLER   Six and a quarter.

CURLY   I don't figger 'at's quite enough, do you?

JUD   It's more'n *you* got.

CURLY   Got a saddle here cost me thirty dollars.

JUD   Yo' cain't bid saddles. Got to be cash.

CURLY (*Looking around*)   Thirty-dollar saddle must be worth sumpin to somebody.

TOM   I'll give you ten.

SKIDMORE (*To* CURLY)   Don't be a fool, boy. Y'cain't earn a livin' 'thout a saddle.

CURLY (*To* TOM)   Got cash?

TOM   Right in my pocket.
        (CURLY *gives him the saddle.*)

CURLY (*Turning to* JUD)   Don't let's waste time. How high you goin'?

JUD   Higher'n you—no matter whut!

CURLY (*To* AUNT ELLER)   Aunt Eller, I'm biddin' all of this ten dollars Tom jist give me.

AUNT ELLER Ten dollars—goin' . . .
        (*Pause. General murmur of excited comments.* LAUREY'*s eyes are shining now and her shoulders are straighter.*)

JUD (*Determinedly*)   Ten dollars *and* two bits.

AUNT ELLER   Curly . . .
(*Pause.* CURLY *turns to a group of men.*)

CURLY   Most of you boys know my horse, Dun. She's a—(*He swallows hard*)—a kinda nice horse—gentle and well broke.

LAUREY   Don't sell Dun, Curly, it ain't worth it.

CORD ELAM   I'll give you twenty-five fer her!

CURLY (*To* CORD ELAM)   I'll sell Dun to you. (*To* AUNT ELLER) That makes the bid thirty-five, Aunt Eller.

AUNT ELLER (*Tickled to death*)   Curly, yer crazy! But it's all fer the schoolhouse, ain't it? All fer educatin' and larnin'. Goin' fer thirty-five. Goin'—

JUD   Hold on! I ain't finished biddin'! (*He grins fiercely at* CURLY) You jist put up everythin' y'got in the world, didn't yer? Cain't bid the clothes off yer back, cuz they ain't worth nuthin'. Cain't bid yer gun cuz you need that. (*Slowly*) Yes, sir. You need that bad. (*Looking at* AUNT ELLER) So, Aunt Eller, I'm jist as reckless as Curly McLain, I guess. Jist as good at gittin' whut I want. Goin' to bid all I got in the world—all saved fer two years, doin' farm work. All fer Laurey. Here it is! Forty-two dollars and thirty-one cents.
(*He pours the money out of his pocket onto* LAUREY's *hamper.* CURLY *takes out his gun. The crowd gasps.* JUD *backs away.*)

CURLY   Anybody want to buy a gun? You, Joe? Bought it brand new last Thanksgivin'. Worth a lot.

LAUREY   Curly, please don't sell your gun.
   (CURLY *looks at* JOE.)

JOE   Give you eighteen dollars fer it.

CURLY   Sold. (*They settle the deal.* CURLY *turns to* AUNT ELLER)
   That makes my bid fifty-three dollars, Aunt Eller. Anybody
   going any higher?

AUNT ELLER (*Very quickly*)   Goin'—goin'—gone! Whut's the
   matter with you folks? Ain't nobody gonna cheer er nuthin'?
   (*Uncertainly they start to sing "The Farmer and the Cowman."*
   CURLY *and* LAUREY *carry their basket away.* JUD *moves slowly
   toward* CURLY. CURLY *sets the basket down and faces him. The
   singing stops.*)

SKIDMORE (*In his deep, booming voice*)   That's the idy! The cowman and the farmer shud be friends. (*His hand on* JUD*'s shoulder*) You lost the bid, but the biddin' was fair. (*To* CURLY)
   C'mon, cowman—shake the farmer's hand!
   (CURLY *doesn't move a muscle.*)

JUD   Shore, I'll shake hands. No hard feelin's, Curly.
   (*He goes to* CURLY, *his hand outstretched. After a pause,* CURLY
   takes his hand, but never lets his eyes leave JUD*'s.*)

SKIDMORE   That's better.
   (*The* PEDDLER *has come downstage and is watching* JUD
   narrowly.)

JUD (*With a badly assumed manner of camaraderie*)   Say, Curly, I
   want to show you sumpin. (*He grins*) 'Scuse us, Laurey. (*Taking*

CURLY's *arm, he leads him aside*) Ever see one of these things?
(*He takes out "The Little Wonder." The* PEDDLER *is in a
panic.*)

CURLY   Jist whut *is* that?
(*The* PEDDLER *rushes to* AUNT ELLER *and starts to whisper in
her ear.*)

JUD   Something special. You jist put this up to yer eye like this,
see?
(CURLY *is about to look when* AUNT ELLER's *voice rings out,
sharp and shrill.*)

AUNT ELLER   Curly! Curly, whut you doin'?
(CURLY *turns quickly. So does* JUD, *giving an involuntary grunt
of disappointment.*)

CURLY   Doin'? Nuthin' much. Whut you want to squeal at a man
like 'at fer? Skeer the liver and lights out of a feller.

AUNT ELLER   Well then, stop lookin' at those ole French pitchers and ast me fer a dance. You brung me to the party, didn't
you?

CURLY   All right then, you silly ole woman, I'll dance 'th you.
Dance you all over the meadow, you want!

AUNT ELLER   Pick 'at banjo to pieces, Sam!
(*And the dance is on. Everyone is dancing now.* WILL *takes*
ADO ANNIE *by the waist and swings her around.* JUD *finally
snaps the blade of "The Little Wonder" back, slips it into his
pocket, then goes up to* LAUREY, *who has started to dance with*

the PEDDLER. *He pushes the* PEDDLER *away and dances* LAU-REY *off.* WILL *and* ADO ANNIE *dance off. The curtains close. Immediately,* WILL *and* ADO ANNIE *dance on to center stage. He stops dancing. They're alone in a secluded spot now, and he wants to "settle things."*)

WILL   Well, Ado Annie, I got the fifty dollars cash, now you name the day.

ADO ANNIE   August fifteenth.

WILL   Why August fifteenth.

ADO ANNIE (*Tenderly*)   That was the first day I was kissed.

WILL (*His face lighting up*)   Was it? I didn't remember that.

ADO ANNIE   You wasn't there.

WILL   Now looka here, we gotta have a serious talk. Now that you're engaged to me, you gotta stop havin' fun! . . . I mean with other fellers. (*Sings*)

You'll have to be a little more stand-offish
When fellers offer you a buggy ride.

ADO ANNIE

I'd give a imitation of a crawfish
And dig myself a hole where I c'n hide.

WILL

I heared how you was kickin' up some capers

When I was off in Kansas City, Mo.

(*More sternly*)

I heared some things you couldn't print in papers

From fellers who been talkin' like they know!

ADO ANNIE

Foot!

I only did the kind of things I orta—sorta

To you I was as faithful as c'n be—fer me.

Them stories 'bout the way I lost my bloomers—Rumors!

A lot o' tempest in a pot o' tea!

WILL

The whole thing don't sound very good to me—

ADO ANNIE

Well, y'see—

WILL (*Breaking in and spurting out his pent-up resentment at a great injustice*)

I go and sow my last wild oat!

I cut out all shenanigans!

I save my money—don't gamble er drink

In the back room down at Flannigan's!

I give up lotsa other things

A gentleman never mentions—

But before I give up any more,

I wanta know your intentions!

With me it's all er nuthin'!

Is it all er nuthin' with you?

It cain't be "in between"

It cain't be "now and then"
No half-and-half romance will do!
I'm a one-woman man,
Home-lovin' type,
All complete with slippers and pipe.
Take me like I am er leave me be!
If you cain't give me all, give me nuthin'—
And nuthin's whut you'll git from me!
   (*He struts away from her.*)

ADO ANNIE
   Not even sumpin?

WILL
   Nothin's whut you'll git from me!
   (*Second refrain. He starts to walk away, nonchalantly. She follows him*)

ADO ANNIE
   It cain't be "in between"?

WILL
   Uh-uh.

ADO ANNIE
   It cain't be "now and then"?

WILL
   No half-and-half romance will do!

ADO ANNIE
   Would you build me a house,

All painted white,
Cute and clean and purty and bright?

WILL

Big enough fer two but not fer three!

ADO ANNIE

Supposin' 'at we should have a third one?

WILL (*Barking at her*)
He better look a lot like me!

ADO ANNIE (*Skeered*)
The spit an' image!

WILL

He better look a lot like me!
(*Two girls come on and do a dance with* WILL *in which they lure him away from* ADO ANNIE. ADO ANNIE, *trying to get him back, does an oriental dance.* WILL, *accusing her, says: "That's Persian!" and returns to the girls. But* ADO ANNIE *yanks him back. The girls dance off.* ADO ANNIE *sings:*)

ADO ANNIE

With you it's all er nuthin'—
All fer you and nuthin' fer me!
But if a wife is wise
She's gotta realize
That men like you are wild and free.
(WILL *looks pleased*)
So I ain't gonna fuss,
Ain't gonna frown,

Have your fun, go out on the town,
Stay up late and don't come home till three,
And go right off to sleep if you're sleepy—
There's no use waitin' up fer me!

WILL

Oh, Ado Annie!

ADO ANNIE

There's no use waitin' up fer me!

WILL

Come on and kiss me!
(ADO ANNIE *comes dancing back to* WILL. *They kiss and dance off.*)

Blackout

Scene II

SCENE: *The kitchen porch of* SKIDMORE's *ranch house. There are a few benches on the porch and a large coal stove.*

The music for the dance can still be heard off stage. Immediately after the curtain rises, JUD *dances on with* LAUREY, *then stops and holds her. She pulls away from him.*

LAUREY Why we stoppin'? Thought you wanted to dance?

JUD Want to talk to you. Whut made you slap that whip onto Old Eighty, and nearly make her run away? Whut was yer hurry?

LAUREY 'Fraid we'd be late fer the party.

JUD You didn't want to be with me by yerself—not a minnit more'n you had to.

LAUREY Why, I don't know whut you're talking about! I'm with you by myself now, ain't I?

JUD You wouldn'ta been, you coulda got out of it. Mornin's you stay hid in yer room all the time. Nights you set in the front room, and won't git outa Aunt Eller's sight. . . . Last time I see you alone it was winter 'th the snow six inches deep in drifts when I was sick. You brung me that hot soup out to the smokehouse and give it to me, and me in bed. I hadn't shaved in two days. You ast me 'f I had any fever and you put your hand on my head to see.

LAUREY (*Puzzled and frightened*)   I remember . . .

JUD   Do you? Bet you don't remember as much as me. I remember eve'ything you ever done—every word you ever said. Cain't think of nuthin' else. . . . See? . . . See how it is? (*He attempts to hold her. She pushes him away*) I ain't good enough, am I? I'm a h'ard hand, got dirt on my hands, pig-slop. Ain't fitten to tetch you. You're better, so much better. Yeah, we'll see who's better—Miss Laurey. Nen you'll wisht you wasn't so free 'th yer airs, you're sich a fine lady. . . .

LAUREY (*Suddenly angry and losing her fear*)   Air you making threats to me? Air you standing there tryin' to tell me 'f I don't 'low you to slobber over me like a hog, why, you're gonna do sumpin 'bout it? Why, you're nothin' but a mangy dog and somebody orta shoot you. You think so much about being a h'ard hand. Well, I'll jist tell you sumpin that'll rest yer brain, Mr. Jud. You ain't a h'ard hand fer me no more. You c'n jist pack up yer duds and scoot. Oh, and I even got better idys'n that. You ain't to come on the place again, you hear me? I'll send yer stuff any place you say, but don't you's much 's set foot inside the pasture gate or I'll sic the dogs onto you!

JUD (*Standing quite still, absorbed, dark, his voice low*)   Said yer say! Brought it on yerself. (*In a voice harsh with an inner frenzy*) Cain't he'p it. Cain't never rest. Told you the way it was. You wouldn't listen—

    (*He goes out, passes the corner of the house and disappears.*
    LAUREY *stands a moment, held by his strangeness, then she starts*

toward the house, changes her mind and sinks onto a bench, a frightened little girl again.)

LAUREY (*There is a noise off stage.* LAUREY *turns, startled*)   Who's 'at?

WILL (*Entering*)   It's me, Laurey. Hey, have you seen Ado Annie? She's gone agin.
(LAUREY *shakes her head.*)

LAUREY (*Calling to him as he starts away*)   Will! . . . Will, could you do sumpin fer me? Go and find Curly and tell him I'm here.
(CURLY *enters*) I wanta see Curly awful bad. Got to see him.

CURLY   Then whyn't you turn around and look, you crazy womern?

LAUREY (*With great relief*)   Curly!

WILL   Well, you found yours. Now I gotta look fer mine.
(*He exits.*)

CURLY   Now whut on earth is ailin' the belle of Claremore? By gum, if you ain't cryin'!
(LAUREY *leans against him.*)

LAUREY   Curly—I'm afraid, 'fraid of my life!

CURLY (*In a flurry of surprise and delight*)   Jumpin' toadstools!
(*He puts his arms around* LAUREY, *muttering under his breath*)
Great Lord!

LAUREY   Don't you leave me. . . .

CURLY   Great Godamighty!

LAUREY   Don't mind me a-cryin', I cain't he'p it. . . .

CURLY   Cry yer eyes out!

LAUREY   Oh, I don't know whut to do!

CURLY   Here. I'll show you. (*He lifts her face and kisses her. She puts her arms about his neck*) My goodness! (*He shakes his head as if coming out of a daze, gives a low whistle, and backs away*) Whew! 'Bout all a man c'n stand in public! Go 'way from me, *you!*

LAUREY   Oh, you don't like me, Curly—

CURLY   Like you? My God! Git away from me, I tell you, plumb away from me!
(*He backs away and sits on the stove.*)

LAUREY   Curly! You're settin' on the stove!

CURLY (*Leaping up*)   Godamighty! (*He turns around, puts his hand down gingerly on the lid*) Aw! 'S cold's a hunk of ice!

LAUREY   Wisht it ud burnt a hole in yer pants.

CURLY (*Grinning at her, understandingly*)   You do, do you?

LAUREY (*Turning away to hide her smile*)   *You* heared me.

CURLY Laurey, now looky here, you stand over there right whur you air, and I'll set over here—and you tell me whut you wanted with me.

LAUREY (*Grave again*) Well—Jud was here. (*She shudders*) He skeered me . . . he's crazy. I never saw nobody like him. He talked wild and he threatened me. So I—I f'ard him! I wisht I hadn'ta! They ain't no tellin' whut he'll do now!

CURLY You f'ard him? Well then! That's all they is to it! Tomorrow, I'll get you a new h'ard hand. I'll stay on the place myself tonight, 'f you're nervous about that hound-dog. Now quit yer worryin' about it, er I'll spank you. (*His manner changes. He becomes shy. He turns away unable to meet her eyes as he asks the question*) Hey, while I think of it—how—how 'bout marryin' me?
(LAUREY, *confused, turns too. They are back to back.*)

LAUREY Gracious, whut'd I wanta marry you fer?

CURLY Well, couldn't you mebbe think of some reason why you might?

LAUREY I cain't think of none right now, hardly.

CURLY (*Following her*) Laurey, please, ma'am—marry me. I—don't know whut I'm gonna do if you—if you don't.

LAUREY (*Touched*) Curly—why, I'll marry you—'f you want me to. . . .
(*They kiss.*)

CURLY   I'll be the happiest man alive soon as we're married. Oh, I got to learn to be a farmer, I see that! Quit a-thinkin' about th'owin' the rope, and start in to git my hands blistered a new way! Oh, things is changin' right and left! Buy up mowin' machines, cut down the prairies! Shoe yer horses, drag them plows under the sod! They gonna make a state outa this, they gonna put it in the Union! Country-a-changin', got to change with it! Bring up a pair of boys, new stock, to keep up 'th the way things is goin' in this here crazy country! Now I got you to he'p me—I'll 'mount to sumpin yit! Oh, I 'member the first time I ever seen you. It was at the fair. You was a-ridin' that gray filly of Blue Starr's, and I says to someone—"Who's that skinny little thing with a bang down on her forehead?"

LAUREY   Yeow, I 'member. You was riding broncs that day.

CURLY   That's right.

LAUREY   And one of 'em th'owed you.

CURLY   That's— Did not th'ow me!

LAUREY   Guess you jumped off, then.

CURLY   Shore I jumped off.

LAUREY   Yeow, you shore did.
       (*He kisses her.*)

CURLY (*Shouting over music*)   Hey! 'F there's anybody out around this yard 'at c'n hear my voice, I'd like fer you to know that Laurey Williams is my girl.

LAUREY   Curly!

CURLY   And she's went and got me to ast her to marry me!

LAUREY   They'll hear you all the way to Catoosie!

CURLY   Let 'em! (*Singing*)
Let people say we're in love!
   (*Making a gesture with his arm*)
Who keers whut happens now!

LAUREY (*Reaching out, grabbing his hand and putting it back in hers*)
Jist keep your hand in mine.
Your hand feels so grand in mine—

BOTH
Let people say we're in love!
Starlight looks well on us,
Let the stars beam from above,
Who cares if they tell on us?
Let people say we're in love!
   (*The curtains close. In front of curtain, the* PEDDLER *walks on, with* ADO ANNIE.)

PEDDLER   I'll say good-bye here, Baby.

ADO ANNIE   Cain't y'even stay to drink to Curly and Laurey?

PEDDLER (*Shaking his head*)   Time for the lonely gypsy to go back to the open road.

ADO ANNIE   Wisht I was goin'—nen you wouldn't be so lonely.

PEDDLER   Look, Ado Annie, there is a man I know who loves you like nothing ever loved nobody.

ADO ANNIE   Yes, Ali Hakim.

PEDDLER   A man who will stick to you all your life and be a regular Darby and Jones. And that's the man for you—Will Parker.

ADO ANNIE (*Recovering from surprise*)   Oh . . . yeh . . . well, I like Will a lot.

PEDDLER   He is a fine fellow. Strong like an ox. Young and handsome.

ADO ANNIE   I love him, all right, I guess.

PEDDLER   Of course you do! And you love those clear blue eyes of his, and the way his mouth wrinkles up when he smiles—

ADO ANNIE   Do you love him too?

PEDDLER   I love him because he will make my Ado Annie happy. (*Taking her in his arms*) Good-bye, my baby. I will show you how we say good-bye in Persia.
(*He draws her tenderly to him and plants a long kiss on her lips.*)

ADO ANNIE (*Wistfully as he releases her*)   That was good-bye?

PEDDLER (*His arms still around her*)   We have an old song in Persia.
It says: (*Singing*)
One good-bye—
(*Speaking*)—is never enough.
(*He kisses her again.* WILL *enters and stands still and stunned.
He slowly awakes to action and starts moving toward them, but
then the* PEDDLER *starts to talk and* WILL *stops again, surprised
even more by what he hears than by what he saw*)
I am glad you will marry such a wonderful man as this Will
Parker. You deserve a fine man and you got one.
(WILL *is almost ashamed of his resentment.*)

ADO ANNIE (*Seeing* WILL *for the first time*)   Hello, Will. Ali Hakim
is sayin' good-bye.

PEDDLER   Ah, Will! I want to say good-bye to you, too.
(*Starting to embrace him.*)

WILL   No, you don't. I just saw the last one.

PEDDLER (*Patting* WILL *on the cheek*)   Ah, you were made for each
other! (*He pulls* ADO ANNIE *close to him with one arm, and puts
the other hand affectionately on* WILL'*s shoulder*) Be good to her,
Will. (*Giving* ADO ANNIE *a squeeze*) And you be good to him!
(*Smiling disarmingly at* WILL) You don't mind? I am a friend
of the family now?
(*He gives* ADO ANNIE *a little kiss.*)

WILL   Did you say you was goin'?

PEDDLER   Yes. I must. Back to the open road. A poor gypsy.

Good-bye, my baby—(*Smiling back at* WILL *before he kisses* ADO ANNIE, *pointing to himself*) Friend of the family. I show you how we say good-bye in my country. (ADO ANNIE *gets set for that old Persian good-bye again. The* PEDDLER *finally releases her and turns back to* WILL) Persian good-bye. Lucky fellow! I wish it was me she was marrying instead of you.

WILL   It don't seem to make no difference hardly.

PEDDLER   Well, back to the open road, the lonely gypsy.
(*He sings a snatch of the Persian song as he exits.*)

WILL   You ain't goin' to think of that ole peddler any more, air you?

ADO ANNIE   'Course not. Never think of no one less'n he's with me.

WILL   Then I'm never goin' to leave yer side.

ADO ANNIE   Even if you don't, even if you never go away on a trip er nuthin', cain't you—onct in a while—give me one of them Persian good-byes?

WILL   Persian good-bye? Why, that ain't nuthin' compared to a Oklahoma hello!
(*He wraps her up in his arms and gives her a long kiss. When he lets her go, she looks up, supreme contentment in her voice.*)

ADO ANNIE   Hello, Will!

Blackout

Scene III

SCENE: *Back of* LAUREY's *house. Shouts, cheers and laughter are heard behind the curtain, continuing as it rises.*

CARNES *and* IKE *walk down toward the house.* CARNES *carries a lantern.*

IKE Well, Andrew, why ain't you back of the barn getting' drunk with us? Never see you stay so sober at a weddin' party.

CARNES Been skeered all night. Skeered 'at Jud Fry ud come up and start for Curly.

IKE Why, Jud Fry's been out of the territory for three weeks.

CARNES He's back. See him at Claremore last night, drunk as a lord!
(*Crowd starts to pour in.* IKE *and* CARNES, *continuing their conversation, are drowned out by the shouts and laughter of the crowd as they fill the stage.* LAUREY *wears her mother's wedding dress. The following lines are sung.*)

AUNT ELLER
They couldn't pick a better time to start in life!

IKE
It ain't too early and it ain't too late.

CURLY

Startin' as a farmer with a brand-new wife—

LAUREY

Soon be livin' in a brand-new state!

ALL

Brand-new state
Gonna treat you great!

FRED

Gonna give you barley,
Carrots and pertaters—

CORD ELAM

Pasture for the cattle—

CARNES

Spinach and termayters!

AUNT ELLER

Flowers on the prairie where the June bugs zoom—

IKE

Plen'y of air and plen'y of room—

FRED

Plen'y of room to swing a rope!

AUNT ELLER

Plen'y of heart and plen'y of hope. . . .

CURLY
> Oklahoma,
> Where the wind comes sweepin' down the plain,
> And the wavin' wheat
> Can sure smell sweet
> When the wind comes right behind the rain.
> Oklahoma,
> Every night my honey lamb and I
> Sit alone and talk
> And watch a hawk
> Makin' lazy circles in the sky.
> We know we belong to the land,
> And the land we belong to is grand!
> And when we say:
> Ee-ee-ow! A-yip-i-o-ee-ay!
> We're only sayin',
> "You're doin' fine, Oklahoma!
> Oklahoma, O.K.!"
> (*The full company now joins in a refrain immediately following this one, singing with infectious enthusiasm. A special and stirring vocal arrangement.*)

CURLY (*After number*)   Hey! Y'better hurry into that other dress! Gotta git goin' in a minnit!

AUNT ELLER   You hurry and pack yer own duds! They're layin' all over my room.

CURLY   Hey, Will! Would you hitch the team to the surrey fer me?

WILL   Shore will! Have it up in a jiffy!

(WILL *runs off.* CURLY *exits into house.* CORD ELAM *runs over to door. The manner of the group of men that surrounds the door becomes mysterious. Their voices are low and their talk is punctuated with winks and nudges.*)

IKE (*To* CORD ELAM)   He's gone upstairs.

CORD ELAM   Yeah.
(*The girls cross to men, but are shooed away. The men whisper and slip quietly off, except for* CARNES.)

ADO ANNIE   Whut you goin' to do, Paw? Give Laurey and Curly and shivoree? I wisht you wouldn't.

CARNES   Aw, it's a good old custom. Never hurt anybody. You women jist keep outa the way. Vamoose!

ADO ANNIE   It ain't goin' to be rough, is it?

CARNES   Sh! Stop gabbin' about it!
(CARNES *exits, leaving only women on the stage.*)

ADO ANNIE   Seems like they's times when men ain't got no need for womern.

SECOND GIRL   Well, they's times when womern ain't got no need fer men.

ADO ANNIE   Yeow, but who wants to be dead?
(GERTIE's *well-known laugh is heard off stage.*)

ELLEN   Gertie!
(GERTIE *enters.*)

ADO ANNIE   Thought you was in Bushyhead.

GERTIE (*Obviously having swallowed a canary*)   Jist come from there.

ELLEN   Too bad you missed Laurey's wedding.

GERTIE   Been havin' one of my own.

ELLEN   Lands! Who'd you marry? Where is he?

ADO ANNIE (*Looking off stage*)   Is that him?

GERTIE (*Triumphantly*)   That's him!
(*All look off right. The* PEDDLER *enters, dejected, sheepish, dispirited, a ghost of the man he was.*)

ADO ANNIE   Ali Hakim!

PEDDLER (*In a weak voice*)   Hello. Hello, Ado Annie.

GERTIE   Did you see my ring, girls?
(*The girls surround* GERTIE *to admire and exclaim. The* PEDDLER *and* ADO ANNIE *are left apart from the group.*)

ADO ANNIE   How long you been married?

PEDDLER   Four days. (GERTIE'*s laugh is heard from the group. He winces*) Four days with that laugh should count like a golden wedding.

ADO ANNIE   But if you married her, you musta wanted to.

PEDDLER   Sure I wanted to. I wanted to marry her when I saw the moonlight shining on the barrel of her father's shotgun! I thought it would be better to be alive. Now I ain't so sure.

GERTIE (*Coming out of group*)   Ali ain't goin' to travel around the country no more. I decided he orta settle down in Bushyhead and run Papa's store.
(WILL *enters.*)

ADO ANNIE   Hey, Will! D'you hear the news? Gertie married the peddler?

WILL (*To* PEDDLER)   Mighty glad to hear that, peddler man. (*Turning to* GERTIE, *and getting an idea*) I think I orta kiss the bride. (*He goes toward* GERTIE, *then looks back at* PEDDLER) Friend of the family . . . remember? (*He gives* GERTIE *a big kiss, not realizing that it is* ADO ANNIE *and not the* PEDDLER *he is burning*) Hey, Gertie, have you ever had a Oklahoma hello?
   (*He plants a long one on* GERTIE. ADO ANNIE *pulls her away and stands in her place.* ADO ANNIE *socks* WILL, *then* GERTIE. GERTIE *strikes back.* WILL *comes between them but is beaten off by both of them. Kicking and slugging, the women resume the fight until* GERTIE *retreats, with* ADO ANNIE *close on her heels. The other girls follow.* WILL, *too, is about to go after them when he is called back by the* PEDDLER.)

PEDDLER   Hey! Where you goin'?

WILL   I'm goin' to stop Ado Annie from killin' yer wife.

PEDDLER (*Grabbing* WILL'*s arm*)   Mind yer own business!
   (*He leads* WILL *off. The stage is empty and quiet. A man sneaks*

on, then another, then more. Cautiously they advance on the house. One of the more agile climbs up a trellis and looks in the window of the second floor. He suppresses a laugh, leans down and reports to the others. There are suppressed giggles and snorts. He takes another peek, then comes down and whispers to them. The joke is passed from one to the other; they are doubled up with laughter. At a signal from one, they all start to pound on tinpans with spoons and set up a terrific din.)

AUNT ELLER (*Coming to the window with a lamp in her hand*)   Whut you doin' down there, makin' all that racket, you bunch o' pig-stealers?

FRED (*Shouting up*)   Come on down peaceable, Laurey sugar!

IKE   And you, too, you curly-headed cowboy.

CORD ELAM   With the dimple on yer chin!

IKE   Come on, fellers, let's git 'em down!
(*Three of the men run into the house. Those outside toss up rag dolls.*)

MEN
Hey, Laurey! Here's a girl baby fer you!
And here's a baby boy!
Here's twins!
(CURLY *is pulled from the house and hoisted on the shoulders of his friends.* LAUREY *and* AUNT ELLER *come out of the house. All are in high spirits. It is a good-natured hazing. Now* JUD *enters. Everyone becomes quiet and still, sensing trouble.*)

JUD   Weddin' party still goin' on? Glad I ain't too late. Got a present fer the groom. But first I wanta kiss the bride. (*He grabs* LAUREY. CURLY *pulls him off*) An' here's my present fer you! (*He socks* CURLY. *The fight starts, with the crowd moving around the two men.* JUD *pulls out a knife and goes for* CURLY. CURLY *grabs his arm and succeeds in throwing him.* JUD *falls on his knife, groans and lies still. The crowd surges toward his motionless body.*)

CURLY   Look— Look at him! Fell on his own knife. (*He backs away, shaken, limp. Some of the men bend over the prostrate form.*)

MEN
Whut's the matter?
Don't you tetch it!
Turn him over—
He's breathin', ain't he?
Feel his heart.
How'd it happen?

FRED   Whut'll we do? Ain't he all right?

SLIM   'S he jist stunned?

CORD ELAM   Git away, some of you. Let me look at him. (*He bends down, the men crowding around. The women, huddled together, look on, struck with horror.* CURLY *has slumped back away from the crowd like a sick man.* LAUREY *looks at* CURLY, *dazed, a question in her eyes.*)

LAUREY   Curly—is he—?

CURLY Don't say anythin'.

LAUREY It cain't be that-a-way.

CURLY I didn't *go* to.

LAUREY *Cain't be!* Like that—to happen to us.

CORD ELAM (*Getting up*) Cain't do a thing now. Try to get him to a doctor, but I don't know—

MAN Here, some of you, carry him over to my rig. I'll drive him over to Doctor Tyler's.

CORD ELAM Quick! I'm 'fraid it's too late.
(*The men lift* JUD *up*.)

MEN
    Handle him easy!
    Don't shake him!
    Hold on to him, careful there!
    (*A woman points to* JUD, *being carried off*. IKE *and his companions run up and exit with the other men*.)

CURLY (*To* LAUREY *and* AUNT ELLER) I got to go see if there's anythin' c'n be done fer him. (*He kisses* LAUREY) Take keer of her, Aunt Eller.
    (*He exits*.)

AUNT ELLER Mebbe it's better fer you and Curly not to go 'way tonight.
    (*She breaks off, realizing how feeble this must sound*.)

LAUREY (*As if she hadn't heard* AUNT ELLER)   I don't see why this had to happen, when everythin' was so fine.

AUNT ELLER   Don't let yer mind run on it.

LAUREY   Cain't fergit, I tell you. Never will!

AUNT ELLER   'At's all right, Laurey baby. If you cain't fergit, jist don't try to, honey. Oh, lots of things happens to folks. Sickness, er bein' pore and hungry even—bein' old and afeared to die. That's the way it is—cradle to grave. And you can stand it. They's one way. You gotta be hearty, you got to be. You cain't deserve the sweet and tender things in life less'n you're tough.

LAUREY   I—I wisht I was the way you are.

AUNT ELLER   Fiddlesticks! Scrawny and old? You couldn't h'ar me to be the way I am!
(LAUREY *laughs through her tears.*)

LAUREY   Oh, whut ud I do 'thout you, you're sich a crazy!

AUNT ELLER (*Hugging* LAUREY)   Shore's you're borned!
(*She breaks off as* CURLY *enters with* CORD ELAM, CARNES *and a few others. Their manner is sober. Some of the women come out of the house to hear what the men have to say.*)

CORD ELAM   They're takin' Jud over to Dave Tyler's till the mornin'.

AUNT ELLER   Is he—alive?
(CORD ELAM *shakes his head.*)

CURLY   Laurey honey, Cord Elam here, he's a Fed'ral Marshal, y'know. And he thinks I orta give myself up— Tonight, he thinks.

LAUREY   Tonight!

AUNT ELLER   Why, yer train leaves Claremore in twenty minutes.

CORD ELAM   Best thing is fer Curly to go of his own accord and tell the Judge.

AUNT ELLER (*To* CARNES)   Why, you're the Judge, ain't you, Andrew?

CARNES   Yes, but—

LAUREY (*Urging* CURLY *forward*)   Well, tell him now and git it over with.

CORD ELAM   'T wouldn't be proper. You have to do it in court.

AUNT ELLER   Oh, fiddlesticks. Le's do it here and say we did it in court.

CORD ELAM   We can't do that. That's breaking the law.

AUNT ELLER   Well, le's not break the law. Le's just bend it a little. C'mon, Andrew, and start the trial. We ain't got but a few minnits.

CORD ELAM   Andrew—I got to protest.

CARNES   Oh, shet yer trap. We can give the boy a fair trial without lockin' him up on his weddin' night! Here's the long and short of it. First I got to ask you: Whut's your plea? (CURLY *doesn't answer.* CARNES *prompts him*) 'At means why did you do it?

CURLY   Why'd I do it? Cuz he'd been pesterin' Laurey and I always said some day I'd—

CARNES   Jist a minnit! Jist a minnit! Don't let yer tongue wobble around in yer mouth like 'at. Listen to my question. Whut happened tonight 'at made you kill him?

CURLY   Why, he come at me with a knife and—and—

CARNES   And you had to defend yerself, didn't you?

CURLY   Why, yes—and furthermore . . .

CARNES   Never mind the furthermores—the plea is self-defense— (*The women start to chatter*) Quiet! . . . Now is there a witness who saw this happen?

MEN (*All at once*)
    I seen it.
    Shore did.
    Self-defense all right.
    Tried to stab him 'th a frog-sticker.

CORD ELAM (*Shaking his head*)   Feel funny about it. Feel funny.

AUNT ELLER   And you'll feel funny when I tell yer wife you're carryin' on 'th another womern, won't you?

CORD ELAM   I ain't carryin' on 'th no one.

AUNT ELLER   Mebbe not, but you'll shore feel funny when I tell
yer *wife* you air.
(*Boisterous laughter.*)

CORD ELAM   Laugh all you like, but as a Fed'ral Marshal—

SKIDMORE   Oh, shet up about bein' a marshal! We ain't goin' to
let you send the boy to jail on his weddin' night. We just ain't
goin' to *let* you. So shet up!
(*This firm and conclusive statement is cheered and applauded.*)

SLIM   C'mon, fellers! Let's pull them to their train in Curly's
surrey! We'll be the horses.

CARNES   Hey, wait! I ain't even told the verdick yet!
(*Everything stops still at this unpleasant reminder.*)

CURLY   Well—the verdick's not guilty, ain't it?

CARNES   'Course, but . . .

LAUREY   Well, then *say* it!
(CARNES *starts, but the crowd drowns him out.*)

ALL   Not guilty!
(CURLY *and* LAUREY *run into the house. The rest run out toward
the stable.* CARNES *is left downstage without a court.*)

CARNES   Court's adjourned!
(CARNES *joins* AUNT ELLER, *who has sat down to rest, after all*

this excitement. ADO ANNIE *and* WILL *enter, holding hands soulfully.* ADO ANNIE'*s hair is mussed, and a contented look graces her face.*)

AUNT ELLER   Why, Ado Annie, where on earth you been?

ADO ANNIE   Will and me had a misunderstandin'. But he explained it fine.
(ADO ANNIE *and* WILL *go upstage and now tell-tale wisps of straw are seen clinging to* ADO ANNIE'*s back. Amid shouts and laughter, the surrey is pulled on.*)

IKE   Hey, there, bride and groom, y'ready?

CURLY (*Running out of the house with* LAUREY)   Here we come!
(*The crowd starts to sing lustily, "Oh, What a Beautiful Mornin'."* LAUREY *runs over and kisses* AUNT ELLER. *Then she is lifted up alongside* CURLY. AUNT ELLER *and three girls start to cry. Everyone else sings gaily and loudly.*)

ALL   Oh, what a beautiful day!
(*The men start to pull off the surrey. Everybody waves and shouts.* CURLY *and* LAUREY *wave back.*)

Curtain

Photograph Credits

Page numbers refer to the insert.

Pages 1–6: Courtesy of Rodgers & Hammerstein / Imagem
Music Group

Pages 7–8: RKO Radio Pictures Inc. / Photofest (photographs
by Schuyler Crail)

Pages 10–13: Photographs by Michael Le Poer Trench, ©
Cameron Mackintosh Ltd.

Pages 14–16: © Joan Marcus